Brooks Too Broad For Leaping
A Chronicle From Childhood

Flannery Lewis

Keep Your Card in This Pocket

Books will be issued only on presentation of proper library cards.

Unless labeled otherwise, books may be retained for two weeks. Borrowers finding books marked, defaced or mutilated are expected to report same at library desk; otherwise the last borrower will be held responsible for all imperfections discovered.

The card holder is responsible for all books drawn on this card.

Penalty for over-due books 2c a day plus cost of notices.

Lost cards and change of residence must be reported promptly.

Public Library
Kansas City, Mo.

Keep Your Card in This Pocket

BROOKS TOO BROAD FOR LEAPING

Brooks Too Broad For Leaping

A CHRONICLE FROM CHILDHOOD

By

F L A N N E R Y   L E W I S

NEW YORK

T H E   M A C M I L L A N   C O M P A N Y

1 9 3 8

PRINTED IN THE UNITED STATES OF AMERICA
BY THE STRATFORD PRESS, INC., NEW YORK

FOR MY MOTHER

PRINTED IN THE UNITED STATES OF AMERICA
BY THE STRATFORD PRESS, INC., NEW YORK

FOR MY MOTHER

"By brooks too broad for leaping . . ."

—HOUSMAN.

DEFINITIONS OF CHILDHOOD

Thou hast made him a little lower than the angels.

The childhood shows the man,
As morning shows the day.

—MILTON.

The child is the father of the man.

—WORDSWORTH.

Children are the keys of Paradise.
They alone are good and wise,
Because their thoughts, their very lives are prayer.

—STODDARD.

Why, the world's full of them, and so is heaven—
They are not rare.

—JEAN INGELOW.

Living jewels dropp'd unstained from Heaven.

—POLLOK.

A lovely being, scarcely form'd or moulded,
A rose with all its sweetest leaves yet folded.

—BYRON.

Behold the child, by nature's kindly law,
Pleased with a rattle, tickled with a straw.

—POPE.

Sleep, sleep, happy child,
All creation slept and smil'd;
Sleep, sleep, happy sleep,
While o'er thee thy mother weep.

—BLAKE.

Sweet childish days, that were as long
As twenty days are now.

—WORDSWORTH.

... At first the infant,
   Mewling and puking in the nurse's arms.
And then the whining schoolboy, with his satchel
And shining morning face, creeping like snail
Unwilling to school ...

—SHAKESPEARE.

THE VOICES OF CHILDREN

When I was a child, I spake as a child . . .
When I became a man, I put away childish things.

CHILDREN IN THE SCHOOLYARD:

EXTRAVAGANT EXAMPLE, *on the Thought,*
Vocabulary, and Rhythm of Childhood:
"Would you like to grow up big? Then leave me
now before I kill you."
—Small boy to an offensive friend.

AN EXPLANATION:
"Sand is only to fill the holes in the ground. The
holes were there before the sand. A man brought it
in a truck that said Uh-Uh, like a pig."
—One friend to another.

JEALOUSY HAS AN UGLY HEAD:
"Who wants to have a bag like yours? You don't
think I do, do you? You don't think I'd carry my
books in it? Hah, I wouldn't have it if you gave it
to me. Here, let's fill it with water!"

THE SENSE OF POWER:
"You can't go away when I got my eyes on you.
'Cause if you did, something would come down from
the sky and hit you on the head, bump, bump."
—Small girl speaking to a friend.

PREJUDICE, AND A CHALLENGE THAT BEGAN
A FIGHT:

"Yah, yah, son of a Jew
Shame on you
Shame, shame on you
Yah, yah, nuts to you!

WORDS FOR A CHILDISH GAME:
"Apple core!"
"Barrymore!"
"Who's your friend?"
"Billy Blank."
"Where?"
"Over there!"
"Sock him, or—
I'll sock you with the apple core!"

CHILDREN AT HOME

EXPLANATION, of the Phenomena of Nature
and the Perversity of Height:

"The tree's not so high, but that the sky is
higher."

> *—Small girl addressing two male friends who*
> *could climb a tree that she could not.*

"I like to ride the clouds, even in the wettest
weather." *—Same girl.*

BOY MUSING:

"When I grow up I'm going to go POP POP POP.
And they'll all be dead, all the people, except my
daddy. POP POP POP, won't I, Daddy?"

- x -

"When I grow up I'll be in a big room . . . A big room! A bigger room than this room. That will be my room until I get to Heaven. . . . I got a little room now, a little bitta room. It's a little room everywhere, but that's an awfully big sun today."

CHILDREN RUNNING WILD
Out of the mouths of babes and sucklings.

In Washington Square, New York:
"Gimme a penny! Gimme a penny!
"Gimme a penny! Gimme a penny!
 Mister . . . Go ahead, Mister, give me a penny!"

 "Dirty rat, dirty face!"

Boy by the old North Church in Boston:
From this church, whose walls are eighteen inches thick, Paul Revere received the signal that sent him by horse . . . one by land and two by sea . . . that the Redcoats were coming. . . . Mister, Gimme a penny. Gimme a penny, Mister.

Four small boys on Brooklyn Bridge, looking down at barges carrying scrap iron:
 "Boy, they make bullets out of that!"
 "Sure they do!"
 "War, boy! If there's another war I'd go!"
 "I wouldn't!"
 "I would!"
 "Aw, I wouldn't go."
 "Why not? You gotta die sometime."

Public Schools in the States of California and New York, conversations gathered at random:

BY BOYS:

"Come on, let's kick him in the face!"
"My belly hurts, bellyhurts, bellyhurts."
"Teacher's pet . . . Teacher's pet!"
"He don't play fair."
"Wilbur's my friend. You gotta give him a chance."

BY GIRLS:

"If you think you're so smart, I'll walk with Phyllis."
"Shut up! If you don't shut up—you just better shut up!"
"I wouldn't talk to her. She's got a smell. She smells! If you talk to her you'll smell!"
"I'm going to Marjory's. I *told* you I'm going to Marjory's. Now *shut up!*"
"Go ahead, tell her. See if I care."

Reading an inscription scrawled in wet cement:

" 'June I. Jane', those are funny words. 'June I. Jane.' That's a funny name. All in front. Look, they all scoop down at one end, except one that's in the middle!"

"We seem but to linger in manhood to tell the dreams of our childhood, and they vanish out of memory, ere we learn the language."

—THOREAU.

"I have seen
A curious child, who dwelt upon a tract
Of inland ground, applying to his ear
The convolutions of a smooth-lipped shell,
To which, in silence hushed, his very soul
Listened intensely; and his countenance soon
Brightened with joy, for from within were heard
Murmurings, whereby the monitor expressed
Mysterious union with his native sea."

—WORDSWORTH.

The young gentlemen, according to Fates and Destinies and such odd sayings, the Sisters Three and such branches of learning, is indeed deceased; or, as you would say in plain terms, gone to heaven."

—SHAKESPEARE.

"Let the children play
And sit like flowers upon thy grave
And crown with flowers,—that hardly have
A briefer blooming-tide than they."

—PALGRAVE.

"Backward, flow backward, O Tide of the years!
I am so weary of toil and of tears,—
Toil without recompense, tears all in vain!
Take them, and give me my childhood again!"
—ELIZABETH AKERS ALLEN.

"But still I dream that somewhere there must be
The spirit of a child that waits for me."
—BAYARD TAYLOR.

"I had none of the enjoyments of city-bred children, and less still of that childish wit which is sure to win maternal admiration for every word that falls from the lips of the little deities. Mother Nature alone gave me a welcome, and yet my early days were not sad; all the countryside looked so lovely to me."
—MADAME MICHLET.

"I cannot but remember such things were,
That were most precious to me."
—SHAKESPEARE.

For it is false to suppose that a child's sense of beauty is dependent on any choiceness or special fineness, in the objects which present themselves to it, though this indeed comes to be the rule with most of us in later life; earlier, in some degree, we see inwardly; and the child finds for itself, and with unstinted delight, a difference for the sense, in whose whites and reds through the smoke on very homely buildings, and in the gold of the dandelions at the road-side, just beyond the houses, where not a handful of earth is virgin and untouched, in the lack of better ministries to its desire of beauty.

—PATER.

"O memories!
  O past that is!"
—GEORGE ELIOT.

Women know
The way to rear up children (to be just);
They know a simple, merry, tender knack
Of tying sashes, fitting baby-shoes,
And stringing pretty words that make no sense,
And kissing full sense into empty words;
Which things are corals to cut life upon,
Although such trifles."
—MRS. BROWNING.

"Twelve years ago I was a boy,
  A happy boy, at Drury's."
—PRAED.

"Here a little child I stand,
  Heaving up my either hand;
  Cold as paddocks though they be,
  Here I lift them up to Thee,
  For a benison to fall
  On our meat and on us all."
—HERRICK.

BROOKS TOO BROAD FOR LEAPING

First Chapter

MEMORY LIVES for such a little while and dies so often that the man could scarcely ever remember what the boy had done. He could not at all recall how the boy looked, or what his smile had been; he could imagine only thin shoulders and freckles, but these were not enough.

The man had just come to the age that he could at times wish he had his life to live over again, in a place he would build from his memory. The nostalgia for dead things was such exquisite pain, and so forbidden, that he found it very pleasant to be rueful. He would be again as he had been as a boy, in that time he fondly determined to be his innocent and carefree childhood, in those days of clear morning before the world had selected him personally to care for its heavy responsibilities.

After all, he had only one life; it was all that was really his; and if that life were his to live, then he would direct it. He would have preferred a second beginning, but if he could not go back to begin once more, he felt that he should at least be able to reflect upon himself as he had been in that time, and to gather from that a reason why he was himself today. That should not be too much to ask.

Yet, even as he tried to penetrate into his refuge, people and causes were closing in all around him. People were shallow and useless, or they were desperate and futile, and everywhere everyone seemed to be waiting for something. Many problems were there whose theories were bristling and turning into action. In other lands, men were killing each other for the right to live; and in all the nations of the world, men with important scowls on their faces made historic and cumbersome speeches, blaming a problem for a universal dilemma, but using one another for the reason to build larger armies, as though there was some secret pact in the high posts, put together with the determination to retain one life by ending another.

Even in his own country, in many familiar places, men in his image, no older, no brighter, no worse than himself, gathered together to beat each other over the head because some lacked enough food to live and others believed they did not need that much. The world itself, spinning around and around the same as ever, seemed wonderfully unconcerned about the whole matter. Suddenly it was as though the people had been placed on the earth and then forgotten, like children left to keep a neglected house.

With this kind of heavenly neglect and individual agitation all around him, the man of this story, who regarded himself as important at least to his own person, feared that a crisis had come. He must declare himself; he must stand manfully upon his side of the battle, or he must at once retreat to a safe place, and the safest place he knew was his childhood.

Like the child, with whom he still shared the first impulses, he wanted to forsake his wooden sword and to run. But escape was no longer that easy. His retreat depended upon memory; and try as hard as he could, he could scarcely remember a thing. He vaguely remembered, or more likely, imagined, something about love and fairness, and a hardset knowledge of right and wrong. But that, too, was probably wish-fulfillment, for when he was confronted with the photographs of the*young, thin, and but partially toothed thing that was himself a while ago, the refuge he had built with such care began to crumble. He noticed with reasonable alarm that the boy's legs, for all of their seven years, seemed to tremble like a puppy's and that his face had such an eager and happy expression, that if he only had a tail, he would have surely wagged it.

This could not be the sprouting seed, the acorn of the oak; this was not the sturdy child, grave with innocence, the father of the man, that he had tried to remember, that indeed he wished to be again; this, with the match-stick body, clothed in the soldier suit, the pinched-face below a mother's idea of an army hat—this child was no closer than a friendly stranger.

Yet, as he studied the photographs in detail, becoming more preoccupied than he should be in such faraway matters, his anticipation became no greater, but his disappointment became something else; and he was aware, after a while, that a great change, even greater than he had thought, had taken place, and still not a great deal had happened.

He did remember distinctly that the world had been better then. The skies were brighter and bluer. The wind was more emotional, the hills were higher, and the sun was so far away that it was clear. The earth itself was more significant. It had depth and it had life. He knew as he walked that underfoot was something deep and alive; and he was convinced at that time there was to everything an earth and a sky, a top and a bottom, a floor and a ceiling, a beginning and an end.

The sky had clouds and mountains. The earth had mountains, too, but they were in the distance. Nearer to him, the earth had cattle and grass, ploughed fields and pine trees. The grass, though, was almost something of its own; it may have been free of either dimension, for it grew wild and green as far as he could see; and, in itself, was so supple, distinct, and strong from the earth that he was always surprised—and sometimes jubilant, and sometimes saddened—that he crushed it as he ran.

Indeed, the world had been better then. The town at that time had no way of knowing that hate would be its keeper. The autumn was yellow and in the sky the fat clouds were as innocent and lazy as cows in their pasture. The changing winds did cause uneasiness, but that was as September warned that winter came closer; and then everyone had work to do, and work has always been capable of dispelling fear.

In the pine forests nearby, the men who could do nothing else, chopped wood, and their sons helped them stack it. The boy could hear the thick sounds of the axes, far away and regular, when the town paused in the evening. Then, even after dark, as lights appeared in the houses, he could sometimes hear a lonely saw complain as it forced its way into a log. Winter was near. He could feel the excitements of its coming.

Everywhere else in the town the heartbeat was almost normal. Crops were good, prices were high; things were not going badly. Already the tempo of living had increased in the cities, but in Colburn in the west, on a foothill that climbed wearily above the Indian River, the things of force and hysteria were real enough, but in the cities, in the crowded places. The tumult was yet to come here, and life now was almost the same as ever.

In the beginning people had come to Colburn for the land. The acres that spread north and south held large ranches that grew crops for the cities; and nearby the ranches, upon land so recently cleared of its timber that the stumps still bled in the spring, were small farms that could support only their families.

The difference to the boy between ranchers and farmers was that when they came to Colburn each week for supplies and to visit, the ranchers drove small automobile trucks, and the farmers came in wagons. Each Saturday morning they were there when the town awakened; Mr. Hobbes found them waiting as he opened the doors of his grocery. Even the boy could tell they were a different people than the merchants.

The ranchers and the farmers, and even the townspeople, too, were much closer to each other than their neighbors to the east of town, the mill men. These men had come later, more than half a century after the discovery of gold, to pick over the remains left by miners; and they were not wanted, for they belonged to the cities and their mills disturbed a land devoted to farming.

The mills were like dredgers, built of large timber scaffoldings, as wide as half an acre, and held great chains of buckets that disappeared into the earth and returned with tons of muddy ore. There were mills of another kind to sift the ore, but they were in the city; the dredgermen never saw the gold they dug.

The dredgermen all looked alike to the boy. Even their houses looked alike. They were built in a community apart from the town; the buildings were small and close together, with the same distance in each house from the front door to the street. These houses were green, exactly the same shade of green, for the company had them all painted at the same time.

The boy saw the dredgermen only when they came to the stores in the evening, and he avoided them, for he heard people say that they were dangerous; they were *an element*; and some of them were lazy and vicious, known as I.W.W.s. He heard that meant "I Won't Work."

He regarded them with grave suspicion. If a dredgerman spoke to him, he ran away, for he did not wish to get into trouble. With his father away, he had a certain responsibility; he must behave himself. That was what his father said. He must also keep care of his mother. That, too, his father had said, looking from him to his mother, was a certain responsibility.

When people asked him if he had heard from his father, the boy was delighted, for usually he had. Addressed to him personally, with his own name on the envelopes, were two letters. "To Master Mark Douglas," they said; he had opened them himself. He had also received four postcards with pictures of white buildings and crooked little streets. But even though they were for him, his mother had to tell him what they said.

"Have you heard from your father, Lad?" Mr.

Hobbes would enquire. And when he said yes, loudly, Mr. Hobbes would say, "And how is his health?" Then he would wink at the boy. "Tell your mother we're sending him a little something my wife made."

With other townspeople it was much the same. The boy liked them and believed them kindly because they were kind to him. They joked with him, and they often teased, for superiority will stoop that far to be replenished. But even when they laughed at him, it was in a friendly fashion. If he could not understand what they meant, he laughed, too, or acted stubborn, whichever way he felt that day. He never knew, in this slight conflict with them, that he held the final thrust, for his helplessness was sharp as the thin weapon of femininity; and he used it quite unconsciously, but over and over again.

To each other, the Colburn people spoke with respect, but with a consciousness of class that required tact, for even though the butcher was not the banker, each in himself demanded his value, and in Colburn that value mattered.

Whether the fathers of the people had hated England or burned witches, whether they had wound over the mountains in prairie schooners and had cleared the land to build their homes; if they lynched Negroes or knew men who shook hands with Lincoln, remembered Concord and the idealists, or knew the sight of gold in the ground—such things could not be told from the lives of their sons, the townspeople. They may have been linked to Europe in family ties or once themselves were ruled by kings; yet in Colburn, in the West, they lived and died in the same dimension, somehow confident and steady, as though the world could fall but they would be safe. They left small marks in their records and newspapers; indeed, an adventure for them was a drive to the city in an automobile, with perhaps Sunday dinner at a new style of restaurant called a *cafeteria*, for in this case, the event was recorded in the Colburn gazette.

How much of this the boy knew then, there is no way of telling. His memory retained images; a snowshed bare in the summertime, an immense man he called Uncle, a parade, a motorcycle and its taste as it passed him, a spotted puppydog, faces in the town, faces everywhere, a party with girls in bright dresses, laughing; these he knew, but they were vague and furtive images, hiding like maidens behind old emotions.

Yet these glimpses were more than sight. They were images with sound and taste and feeling, if that can be; and none came in logical order. Indeed, they might have all been impressed upon him by emotion rather than thought, for they remained in him too fluid and volatile for adult intelligence to rearrange. Words give them a pattern they do not possess, because if childhood feelings have a pattern at all, it is as uncertain and hesitant as the first ripples over unruffled water.

Into the homes that he went with his mother, people sang around the piano, and the song they sang was "Over There." He could sing it himself, and he could sing the other song, "Drink to me only with thine eyes." And at night, in the houses, they said women were doing their part for conscription, suffrage, and prohibition—three words, all flat, that were all alike. And in daytimes they said Buy a Liberty Bond. They read the newspaper and said men were never braver before, and even toward town wildflowers appeared in the spring; in the fall there were berries so vividly red that they smeared your fingers, and all that season there was holly and mistletoe. And down the street came the parades!

Oh! These were exciting days; but the time of the century had not yet been dislocated, for when he was tired, he could lie on his back on the cool lawn to look at the sky. He could stay there forever and see the whole world. People said this and people said that, but it was all the same for him, his mother said, because it went in one ear and out the other.

But his mother was not entirely right. Even though at that time everything was moving, moving like the sky overhead, the boy retained some of the period in this clear fluid of sounds and words and feelings. It was there when the man returned, like water that stays in a well.

For it is true that when you come back to an old house that has been abandoned for years, and try to turn the faucet for a drink you remember from your childhood, the faucet at first refuses to turn; and when it does, with a wrench, the water spurts and pushes backward in the pipe. It is rusty and has a faint smell of old dust, but when you let it run long enough, the water comes freely and clean; and after that, while you use the faucet, the water is always there whenever you want it.

Memory, too, has that quality; but with a child there is another difficulty, for events come so quickly around him that his memory could be compared to a moment that has many sounds, in which no one predominates. Nothing, then, that happened in the childhood of this boy Mark had clarity or order until the year came along that he started to school; he must have been ready for it, and that year must have been very important, for it had a place of its own in his mind, as bright and as clear as the ring of a bell.

He was walking up a steep hill, very early in an autumn morning, with a new notebook and a lunch-box, a blotter, a pen, and pencils enough for a life-time, when he was bravely seven and going to school.

But was he as brave as he thought? Probably not, but it does seem appropriate that the boy should have been fully aware he was marching away that morning to meet the world and that his only glance back should have been over his shoulder. Yet, it may have been only curiosity and a restless eagerness that prodded him with such elation up the steep hill. Of course, to get to the hill from his house, he had to walk down another just as steep, but that was before memory began; and that may be just as well.

There was no kindergarten in this small town; the boy was to begin in the first grade. It must have made him, in his own eyes, more important that he would be in the same school with those accomplished people of thirteen and fourteen years of age, those tall and noisy people whom he respected from afar. He would be one of them, that was his hope, but an adult he would never be, for they moved thoughtfully in a lofty world of their own.

As he walked up the hill he recalled his mother's admonition for him to save his lunch until lunchtime, and to stand up straight, for heaven's sakes. He did stand fairly straight this morning, shoulders back, head up, taking gulps for breath; but all this was later to become an impossibility, or too much bother for doubtful benefits to come.

There was autumn in the air, and he could taste it. He was more aware of the seasons then. Reading and writing had not yet interrupted his gaze at his own limited horizon, and he was sensitive simply because he was doing things for the first time. Soap still hurt his skin, a bath was almost unbearable, and a year would be before his clothes were part of himself.

The sun was faraway but bright this morning and it made a shine on the cement sidewalk. He must have been impressed with the sidewalk and the hill that it rested upon, for they were to become his standards of comparison for all sidewalks and hills. This walk, which was very broad with its fine cement, led to the main street of the town, to the board walks in front of the stores.

Now he must cross the street. First, he must look to the left. Second, to the right. Third, he must listen. If he heard or saw an automobile coming, he must wait; indeed, he had to wait no matter how far one might be . . . But if as far as he could see there was no automobile in sight that was moving— then he could cross the street.

This morning there were many automobiles at the curb, but only people moved. Many flags were flying and most of the people were standing near the railroad depot, in the station yard, all of them talking, as grown-ups so often do, and most of them with a gauze mask across their mouths and noses. He was wearing that kind of a bandage himself. He would have preferred it off his face, but he realized he must never remove it, no matter what happened.

Somehow he seemed to know his way to school. The man had no recollection of the boy ever having been there before, but the boy knew where he was walking; he knew that at the school he would meet Mr. Blake and Miss Matthews. His mother may have led him to school for a visit, when he was younger; and it was likely that his mother wanted to lead him there today, but since she was not with him now, he must have pleaded, as he always did in such situations later, to go alone.

He came to the acorn tree. He was in a hurry and getting excited, but he had to pause. The tree, which may have been large and spreading in the traditional fashion of oak trees, was not at all important; yet the acorns beneath it were. They looked like nuts; he was angry at them when they did not taste good to eat . . . But then he saw something better yet. A white worm was crawling dreamily along the base of the tree. He started to kill it with his hands; but he changed his mind and got a stick instead. He knelt on his knees, carefully balanced the stick, and with it squashed the worm. The back part dropped off first, but the front part wiggled and flopped up and down, until he squashed it, too. It became a green with white dots, which he minutely examined.

Psychologists could have a theory or two for that action, but the boy himself had no way of knowing that he had that moment indicated he was becoming a human being, rather than an animal, that he had changed his mind and used a tool for his killing. Indeed, he was already thinking of other matters. He was appreciating the long line of white picket fences, as he passed the houses on the hill. Perhaps he did no more to the fine line than appreciate it this morning, but he was later to obey some instinct deep and obscure in boys from all time, and likely akin to the urge to press one's foot in fresh cement. The manifestation of that instinct would be for him to hold a pencil in his hand, to make a fine rattling noise as he walked along, and thus, also, to leave his mark as he went his way.

That first journey to school came upon an untoward incident. The boy passed a small pasture, above the town, and surprised a flock of geese. He may have seen geese before, but these were acting especially strange, and he stood there watching them.

But not for long. A gander took a dislike to him and strolled over, becoming more belligerent the nearer he came. He was a very large gander. He made threatening gestures with his dirty white wings; and, when a bone beak he had began to make hissing noises, the boy got ready to run. But he hesitated, almost fascinated, as though he stared into the serpent's eye. Then the gander started for him. Still he hesitated. But when the gander was almost eye to eye with him, the boy found he could stay there no longer; his legs got underway, and he ran as hard as he could, with the gander right behind him, hissing. The boy began to cry, but he held his sobs when he realized that no one but the geese would hear him; besides, he could not run as rapidly with a lump in his throat. The feeling to cry was there, but the tears were not. He opened his mouth wide and tried to run faster, but the gander kept right behind him; and once, he almost gave in—he almost fell to the ground to let the gander get him. He wanted to plead with the gander.

Mark escaped finally, but he was very frightened. When at last he looked around, the gander was about fifty feet away. He leaned against a rock; his lungs were burning and his heart had a hammer in it. He wished to go home, but that would mean passing the geese again. Looking to them, he saw the gander wave his wings in derision and walk rapidly around in a circle; and then he waddled triumphantly back to his geese, who must have received him with a certain admiration.

It was obvious to the boy that the gander, having triumphed, would now ignore him and that henceforward he was safe. That was good, for he had important business this morning; why, he was on his way to school! *He was on his way to school!*

He could see the flags waving on the houses; it was a day for celebration, and up the street, housewives were murmuring over the fences. A little girl with thin legs was walking along with her mother and twittering of events to come. And when at last the boy turned the corner to the school, he could see the other children; and now his heart was beating as wildly as when the gander chased him. He decided he was able to walk a little faster. The bandage across his mouth was in his way, but it was no cause for complaint, less for alarm, for everyone wore one. He had the bandage because people said:

I had a little bird and his name was Enza
I opened the window—and In-flu-enza.

Neither did he really know why the flags were flying or the people talking, and he certainly did not care. He was within a block of the school and coming closer; in a moment he would be there. And, indeed, it was not until a decade later that he read in a book of history that upon that day of September:—

Germany indicated its collapse. Food was scarce, the Imperial Navy was bottled in the harbor at Kiel; while at that time dispatches from abroad stated that Germany itself was beset by revolutionists. Sources close to the Kaiser refused to explain his position; on the same date the Allied Forces began the artillery bombardment for the greatest military drive ever made.

The American command laid a creeping barrage over the German sector which extended back from seven miles. Back and forth, from front to rear, all that day, successive curtains of steel swept the German line, laying waste to entrenchments, crippling communication, and causing casualties the extent of which was never known.

Still, the boy thought that it was a very lovely world, that September morning. The gander was gone and ahead was his destination. In the clear autumn weather he had even then a feeling of sadness and security, and yet in his sadness he was by times jubilant, in a kind of tragic excitement, for here was his new life ahead. The sun had left as the morning lengthened and now the air was so still there was sure to be a storm. He was a long way from home, but he realized suddenly that if it did storm, he would be safe; he would be in school, and he could watch it from a window.

Second Chapter

FOR THE first few mornings there was no doubt but that the schoolbells were ringing especially for him. They gave him a certain elation, a kind of headlong encouragement, these outspoken representatives of wisdom, textbooks, and integrity, ringing over the hillside, catching him as he dawdled or thought of other things. They dispelled his misgivings and ended his fears, like florid and stout little men, reassuring him loudly that everything was going to turn out all right. They invited him onward, in this amiable fashion; and when they bid him come, he was glad to go.

Each morning he would search the schoolyard for his teacher, Miss Matthews; and as likely as not she would be standing by the teeter-totter with a whistle to her lips. The wind would be blowing her yellow hair across her face; she would raise her hand, again and again, to brush it back, while on all sides, as around a maypole, the children gathered in bright excited patches.

Miss Matthews was a very tall young woman, and for that moment she was not only tall, she was monumental. For the boy, she had no age; she was grown up; that was enough. She was his good friend, that was true, too, and yet since that first morning, she had become a figure in a landscape that was slightly foreign to him. He had watched her carefully that day, trying to decide if he should say hello to her; but even as he watched, his presence left him, his imagination departed from his body, and from a distance he began to see her as she really was. She was Miss Matthews, yes, but she was also another person that he knew——a woman called the Statue of Liberty. He knew the Statue well from stamps that his mother purchased for him; they were Liberty Bond stamps, but this he did not know until later, and then it seemed of small importance, for his mother had impressed upon him that it was not the stamps but the story of the Statue that mattered; and the story, which he could not recall at the moment, was that whatever she held aloft in her hand was worth keeping.

Now, in their importance and appearance, he simply confused Miss Matthews with the Statue of Liberty; he realized vaguely, as his mind once more returned to his body, that between the ladies there was a difference; but there was also a strong likeness somewhere, and whenever afterward he regarded either one, they became the same, calm person.

Miss Matthews used to come to his mother's

house to play trains with him on the floor; that, of course, was before she had so suddenly become immortal. She kissed him when she came, and when she left. He did not care for kissing, but if he had to be kissed by anyone except his mother, the person might as well be Miss Matthews. He had not often kissed his father . . . Thinking of his father, he remembered the day clearly that his father left for France. That day hung in space instead of time, but he recalled it now, for Miss Matthews had stayed at his house in the morning while his mother went with his father to the city; she had been very nice to him. There had been a great deal of kissing, and he was glad when the day was done.

Now the boy was afraid that Miss Matthews was going to kiss him again, before all these strangers, on this, his first day of school. She wore no mask; instead she had some sort of a small white bag, like the one lots of people wore, that hung from a loose cord around her neck. He feared that neither the bag nor his mask would be a helpful obstacle if she decided to kiss him. This morning, though, she was a woman of the world, for when her gaze finally descended upon him, she greeted him with a smile and a nod no more confidential than she gave to anyone else. He was at once relieved; still, he must have considered, if at all he loved a gesture, that it would have been indeed fitting this day to begin his career with a kiss from the Goddess of Liberty.

"I want all the new pupils to come over here,"

she kept repeating; and some of them crowded very close to her, indeed, as though they were accustomed to apron strings. But there were others reluctant, perhaps restrained by the same force that withheld the boy, for he felt that Miss Matthews, that monument, had become the center of the world, and that surely all eyes everywhere were upon her. He was usually the center of the world himself, as he had been on his way to school; but now Miss Matthews was the center, and he feared that any movement of his would attract attention to his person. Then he would be the center, too; then all eyes would be upon him. No, it was better to remain completely still. It was better yet to keep his head down and his hands in his pockets; besides, in this reticent position, he could let his eyes look anywhere that they wished.

He found, of a sudden, that he was fond of his eyes; he was unable to put his affection into logic that could be spoken, but his eyes, which never before had commanded his objective interest, were a realized convenience that now had his gratitude. Not so much that they could see, but that they were not hands—or feet, for that matter; that is why he liked them. His hands and feet had been giving him trouble; they moved around, they were restless, they drew attention; they did not know their place. But his eyes . . . he loved them; they might move in their sockets like marbles, but never once did they get in his way.

And there was a good deal this morning that his eyes intended to see. All these children, these strangers, were standing there, a score of them, at least; the girls in their gingham and calico dresses, cotton-wool stockings and sweaters, and the boys in knickers and sweaters, with those kind of shirt waists that have strings to them, those strings which forever insist upon dangling down in front.

The boy seemed impressed with the sight. He watched gravely and listened to the mothers in animated conversation with Miss Matthews, and he noted, but without emotion, that the mothers, with what seemed to him exceptional skill, could pluck forth from the bright patch their own particular child, for teacher's nodding inspection. He was glad for himself that he was not in this manner thrust toward Miss Matthews. He was thinking only of himself, for it failed to occur to him that they were strangely eager, those mothers, to guide away their child's first step.

The children must have been cautioned against protest because they remained quiet and continued profound studies of their own shoes. Yet despite the importance of the occasion, the mothers sometimes had to turn their backs to the teacher to shield their faces from the wind that whirled over the granite-dust schoolyard, to cause such a fuss when it fell upon the sandpile by the teeter-totter.

After one of these pauses, he was surprised to hear his own name called; indeed, he was not at all happy to hear it, for he feared that it would attract attention. But when he looked around the yard, he saw that it was Mr. Blake who had called to him; Mr. Blake was his best friend and he was glad to see him. It was not strange to him that a moment ago he had forgotten Mr. Blake existed.

The boy started to run toward Mr. Blake, and then remembered that people were probably watching. Instead he walked to him as quickly as he could, and Mr. Blake took his hand and led him to the porch, away from the wind.

"Well, Mark," he said, "I'm glad to see you here."

Mark nodded and mumbled to indicate that he was also happy. Mr. Blake was just about the finest man that he knew, excepting his father, of course. But Mark did wish that he was not bald-headed. But bald-headed he was, and thin, too, with high cheek bones and a face so clear that you could see the veins underneath. Not only that, but his shoulders were slender and his wrists were flat, with fingers long and thin. Wherever he was, he seemed always the same, and he walked so straight and had such a solemn appearance that Mark had known him a long time before he enjoyed talking to him. He always wore a brown suit that fitted him precisely, and with it a stiff, white collar. He was always like that, hard and stiff, and as flat as wood; yet Mark liked him, as much and as vaguely as a child can like anyone who lives in that other world.

- 24 -

It had been sometime, though, before Mr. Blake appeared in Mark's mind as an individual and friend, rather than the man who was Judith's father. Judith herself was entering school for the first time that day, but at the moment Mr. Blake seemed more concerned with Mark, but perhaps that was because he was principal of the school and must not reveal too much concern for his own child.

Now Mr. Blake looked at the boy with mock appreciation and talked to him as adults will to a child, carefully, as though a third person were present. "So," he said, "you're a man now, are you?" and he smiled. Mark was glad to agree.

"Well, I'm as proud of you, Mark, as proud as though you were my own son. We're old friends, and you ought to get along fine in school. And you'll get along fine with Miss Matthews; she's your teacher now—remember." Mr. Blake paused; he started to say something else, and the boy stepped back to be able to see his face above his neck. (And occasionally, from the sides of his wonderful eyes, Mark could see flashes of the children in the yard.) But Mr. Blake was saying something to him.

"I meant to tell you, Mark, that you could go to school with Judith and me in the morning, if you wanted to get up half an hour earlier. You can ask your mother about that. Or if you want to, you and Judith can go together a little later."

Mark feared he would not like that, but he did

not say so. Anyway, the morning was too exciting for him to say much. He just liked to look. He could see the children were coming toward the porch.

"All right," said Mr. Blake, and his voice came from a distance, "you just remember that now I'll be a sort of——daddy to you." He put his hand on Mark's shoulder and squeezed him.

Mark felt uncomfortable, for some reason. He did not perceive what Mr. Blake was talking about. Indeed, he seldom did, exactly. But now he felt as though something else new was beginning . . . And suddenly he had an apprehension. Now that he was a pupil, now that the world had a new meaning, now would he and Mr. Blake be able to dig together in the garden?

He wanted to ask, but the children were crowding to the porch and Mr. Blake was nodding and smiling. Mark saw Miss Matthews and she beckoned him to follow. He waved to Mr. Blake, who stood watching him, and——with a held breath——he walked into the classroom.

Once seated, he was eager to see what the room would look like. He was not disappointed; he was quite relieved, for he saw chairs, for one thing, and the sight made him rather happy. There were chairs in his house, too. He had to laugh at the coincidence. They were straightback chairs, they were in the front of the room, and the mothers were sitting in them, with their dresses tucked under their ankles. But a few of the mothers, for whom there were no chairs, looked about the room uncertainly and gave sly glances to the clock.

In all, the room was a pretty fine place, he thought, with its furniture freshly shellacked and its large flag hanging from the wall. That flag, in itself, was worth inspection, for not only was it brightly colored, but on the handle it had a good deal of brass; and on the perch above the handle was a gilt eagle. Teacher's desk was beneath the flag, to face the desks of the pupils. Immediately it became a bear, and as quickly did the other desks turn into cubs.

Around the room ran a blackboard; in one corner, in a brown box, stood the clock. The boy could not tell the time, but he knew what clocks were for, and in the brown days to follow he often watched its hands as they calmly met and separated, met and went their separate ways again.

But of course there were many other things in the room to compel his interest. A pile of blocks in gay colors, but chipped a little, were piled against the blackboard, a tumble-down town in pieces of color against the blackboard mountain; and on the wall, almost all the way around the room, were picture stories of boys and girls, and wolves and grandmothers.

Mark felt better yet when he saw the blocks; he had some of his own. They were like the chairs in their effect, for seeing them made him laugh with delight. Oh, he knew a thing or two about letters!

His blocks had letters, too, with an *A* that led to a *B*, and a *C* that came up in a hurry. It was a lengthy and sometimes a confusing route that led to *M*, but he liked *M* best of all, for *M* began to spell Mark, and Mark was his name. Why, of course; *Mark was his name!* And just thinking of that, made him laugh again.

Behind the classroom was a cloakroom; in a moment it came into importance. When the teacher had completed her discussion with the assembled mothers, she turned to the class and said:

"I am very, very pleased to see all of these bright, sunshiny faces, and I am sure that we are all going to be very good friends, aren't we?"

A murmur of contentment ran around the room; the mothers beamed and nodded. Miss Matthews smiled.

"And I have a real surprise for you this morning . . . a real surprise. After today no one will have to wear his—or her—influenza mask any more! Isn't that fine?"

And fine it was, as everyone said. The teacher held up her hand for the class to listen.

"No, don't remove your masks now, but I am going to give each of you a card from the principal's office. Take it home to your parents—your mothers and fathers, this afternoon. Then tomorrow . . . you can come to class without your masks."

To the mothers she said, "I can't guarantee a treat like that for them every day!" To the class, she said, "Do you all understand what I mean? You bring the cards home to your mothers—your parents—remember, now; and after that you may remove your masks . . .

"There will be a piece about it in the paper this afternoon," she added, and turned to the mothers and nodded. The mothers nodded in return, each smiling hurriedly, in a sweet fashion.

"You know, Children," Miss Matthews said, changing the subject, "that each morning when you come to school, you will come to this room. As you enter the room—that is, as you come in the door—you will walk through that little room back there. That's the cloakroom. And put your hats and coats on a hook. Boys will put their caps there, too," she added, for some of the boys had rolled their caps and stuffed them in their pockets.

"Each pupil," she said, "will have a hook of his own. It's your special hook—and you want to make sure that you use it . . . And today, I am going to ask one boy in each row to take all the fine hats and coats to the cloakroom. Now, which of you boys will do that for us?"

Everyone shouted that he would, in the same wild outcry of delight, for everyone had been sitting silent a very long time and it was good, for a change, to raise one's voice. But the hubbub caused Miss Matthews to look grieved. She raised her hand.

"After this time," she said, "we shan't speak in class until we are spoken to. When we wish to speak, we shall raise our hand. See—like this." And Miss Matthews raised her hand again.

"Now, who would like to take our hats to the cloakroom?"

Everyone raised his hand, but someone forgot and shouted, "Me!" Miss Matthews ignored him. It was fortunately not Mark; although the cry had been in him, it did not come out. But he had tried to raise his hand the highest of all, for it suddenly seemed to him of the utmost importance that he make that trip to the cloakroom. It would be moving; and, besides, he would be doing something for his dear friend, Miss Matthews, the Statue of Liberty.

But the teacher called upon Phillip and Johnny and Perry, and someone else; and Mark was left with his hand high in the air.

Miss Matthews, in fact, seemed to know all the strange names; but the boy had never doubted she would know so much. He simply accepted her knowledge, even though the names were sounds confusing or twisting to him, excepting Richard's; and when Miss Matthews began assigning the pupils their permanent seats, he hoped that she would be canny enough to place him beside Richard. He knew Judith, of course, for not only was she Mr. Blake's daughter, but she was his neighbor to the hill house; however, he did not wish to sit beside her. She was sometimes difficult . . . But he was placed among strangers, between a girl named Margaret and a boy called Peg.

Margaret was a person one never looked at twice, but Peg demanded inspection. Both Peg and Mark gave each other a look. In Mark's eyes there was curiosity and a faint suspicion; after all, Peg was a stranger. He had a nose as round as a button, a thick neck, and he wore a red sweater with a roughneck collar. Mark noticed that he also had brown spots, probably moles, on his face, so he was immediately wary of him. But Peg himself did no more than grin and enquire, "What's your name, guy?"

"My name is Mark," he replied, with some pride. "I live on the hill. What's your name?"

"Puddin'n Tame," said Peg, "Ask me again and I'll tell you the same," and he laughed in a superior fashion, to glance left and right in triumph.

Mark was suddenly puzzled; true, he laughed, but that was because he did not wish to appear ignorant. In his chagrin, though, he was inwardly angry; already had he been outwitted. He had feared something like this. He intended to speak a disparaging comment in revenge. Instead he busied himself placing his pen and pencils in his desk, for his desk was already a kind of home and would later be a stronghold. Then he looked around the room, pretending to be avidly interested in whatever he saw, for by the twitch of his neck he could tell that Peg was watching.

In a moment, though, it was time for Mark to stand with the class and sing a song, which was entitled "Good Morning to You." Miss Matthews maintained the beat with one hand, while the class repeated and sang after her:

> *Good morning to you,*
> *Good morning, dear Teacher,*
> *Good morning to you.*

Then everyone turned to his neighbor. Mark had to make a quick choice between Margaret and Peg; he had to choose Peg, and to him he sang:

> *Good morning to you,*
> *Good morning, dear Classmate,*
> *Good morning to you.*

Three times the class repeated the song and each time Peg had a leer for Mark. Then the song was mastered, after a fashion, despite broken trebles and piping voices. Faces were shining, and to each heart came the belief that school was going to be very fine.

Peg leaned across the aisle to another boy. "I did this all before," he whispered, but loud enough for Mark to hear.

"Did what?" said the other boy, loudly.

"I did this all before, this singing. I started school last year—but I had to quit."

"Why?" the boy whispered.

"Aw, I broke my leg," Peg said, and returned to his desk.

The boy was thunderstruck. Mark, too, whirled around, amazed. *Peg had broken his leg!* Mark looked at him carefully, and breathed deeply. What a hero he must be! He quickly decided he would like to be friends with Peg, and first of all, he wanted to ask him how he had broken it. But he did not get the chance, for the class had to stand again to face the flag and repeat,

"I pledge allegiance to the Flag of the United States . . ."

But that is all of the pledge that Mark ever learned. The rest of it may have been as stirring as a roll of drums, but it was beat in confusion, and all that remained in the boy's mind was something about "Upon my honor, of which I stand . . . one nation indivisible . . ." And whenever afterward he repeated it, he thought how extraordinary it was that he sat beside a boy who had broken his leg.

So it was that the boy had never learned the Pledge of Allegiance, although he repeated it again and again, morning after morning. Years later he was still skipping through it somehow, but never once was he ever struck with the futility of ever trying to learn anything. "Indivisible" remained in his mind, though, as heavy as a log at the bottom of a brook, for it was too much; it could not be lifted; he had not the slightest idea of what it meant.

It did seem to Mark that morning as if he was no sooner reacquainted with his desk than it was a time called recess, and Miss Matthews was explaining what to do when the bell rang.

"At the sound of the bell," she said, "the class will rise and leave the room. If the bell rings while you are outside, come back to the room . . . right away! But remember! walk slowly, do not crowd to the door."

But leaving the room was even more complicated than that. Everyone must *file* out. Mark was to follow Peg and Peg was to follow the boy who sat behind him.

Outside the storm had fallen upon the schoolyard. The air was wet with mist, but the wind was imperious, and its impatience with the autumn leaves kept them tumbling one way and another, until in terror they flattened themselves against the building. The sky had darkened and in the distance thunder clapped in a fearful manner, as if it knew indeed what a fright it could be. On the school porch the girls wriggled in anxiety and looked to one another with happy alarm. And, as suddenly the sky became purple, total strangers wished to clasp one another. Miss Matthews, that unshaken monument, made everyone stand back under the porch, for in the next moment the clouds had opened and the rain came down.

But although exciting the scene, the boy did not this time forget his body. Indeed, he believed the time had come to accomplish something that he had intended for more than an hour. He edged nearer Miss Matthews, who was laying soothing words on an excited outbreak of little girls. He was reluctant to interrupt her, but when she looked his way, he was not bashful as he said, "Miss Matthews, where's the bathroom, please?" and he waited to be told.

A silence fell—a silence louder than the thunder —and then there was one tentative giggle, like the first rain drop, and even before the teacher could reply, there was another, then another; and when she took him by the shoulder and pointed out the boys' lavatory, the girls looked at one another and in rhythm raised their shoulders, to shriek into their handkerchiefs. Mark heard them, all right. And even then he knew that this was his introduction to the behavior of girls, and that it was the way they acted when there was more than one of them to face; and even then he knew that it was not a really good beginning.

As Miss Matthews led him to the door, he heard nothing that she said; he was too busy seeing the scene in retrospect; his good question and the giggle it got. He feared that he surely must have made a great mistake; however, he determined to repeat it never. Next time, in a similar situation, he would be the first to laugh. And he *was* determined, for years later, when a girl asked the teacher where calves came from, anyway, he laughed as loudly as anyone else; although it was true that he did not know the answer then, either.

Back in the schoolroom, the excitement subsided, Mark remembered it was his custom to have a nap before lunch. He arose really early in the morning; this morning he had, indeed, been up very early; more than that, he had not slept well the night before. Dreams of anticipation insisted upon interrupting his rest, and he was worn with their monotony, for in each dream he had attended a rather horrible school in which teachers towered over him like the roof of a house. Now that he was really in school, and found it not unpleasant, he realized that it was increasingly difficult for him to remain awake. He was accustomed to sleeping when he became sleepy, but he did believe that at this time it would be unbecoming for him to sleep at his desk. Yet to remain awake, to keep his attention upon Miss Matthews—that was almost too much to ask, even though he feared that she must be saying something of utmost importance.

But it was deliciously warm in the room. The sky outside was beginning to lighten; the sun was breaking through the clouds, the wind was not as angry as before, and inside the room there was peace. He discovered that his eyes were no longer heavy once they were closed. And, after an experiment, he found it comfortable to cross his arms on his desk and, a moment later, to place his head upon them. He politely remained awake for a moment, but no one discouraged him. And, in another moment, it was too late for anyone to say anything; he was asleep.

How long he slept, he did not know. But the sky lowered gently; the obliging earth came to meet it; there was a wedding. Blue joined red in gentle tumults and peace came upon him. Doves made gentle noises—but then fluttered and were gone, for suddenly a gander complained; and then he heard laughter, Peg's laughter, and from afar an angry voice! The gander was his teacher, and the gander was exceedingly angry!

Mark shook himself in terror. He was awake and inwardly cowering. He had gone to sleep in school —before all these strangers. What would they think of him? Yet all about him was the gentle murmur of voices; Miss Matthews was at the blackboard, and not even looking his way. Perhaps no one had seen him. But had Peg? He whirled in his chair, but not even Peg knew. Peg, however, looked up, so Mark gave him a scowl, anyway; and that started it. They looked at each other levelly and this time curiosity was satisfied, and neither liked what he saw.

Somehow that look began a cycle of incidents. Miss Matthews, the storm, the girls, the flag, and the desk were things of school, interesting, but not much else. But the look was something sinister, Mark feared, for in his mind it took a dark meaning of its own, later related in an odd fashion to all the adversity of his childhood, so that whenever he thought of Peg, he recalled the fight, the note that Judith wrote, and that time, months afterward, when many things happened to the town and people said that the dying turned black in a day. This afternoon itself may have been like any other in the school had it not been for Peg—and had it not been, too, that the boy was concerned with the important fact that when he got home he would have a lot to tell his mother.

Third Chapter

WHEN MARK said that his house was on the hill, he could have added that it was near so many trees that he almost lived in a forest. North and to the south was the farming country, just as east was the Indian River; but on this hill he was at the height of the sloping plateau that led down through the town to the water. The land was west; it was rugged, and often in autumn the wind came there. But his house had its back squarely to the forest, with a high board fence beyond it. In the front, the façade and the porch protected the flowers his mother grew in the garden, and the fence in back protected the apple trees behind the house, so that his place was easily a fortress, built with the seasons in mind.

Mark always knew that he needed the house for his own protection; he could not well forget it, for there was a reminder beyond the fence, an apple tree that faced the wind; in the years it had grown bent, as though the wind held it back, and when he knew the tree it was as crooked and gnarled as a witch on a broom.

The thing he could not understand, though, was why, if the apple tree was crooked, that the pine trees in the forest stood so straight. Perhaps it was because they were so high overhead that they became their own masters; yet, that may not have been true, because there were occasions when even they had to submit to the weather, for nights came when the wind was so imperious that the boy in his bed could hear the pines complaining as they bowed to let the wind go by.

It was always good to return to that house, particularly after school, because when he came within sight of it he would be rehearsing in his mind the story of what happened that day and whether he had won or lost at marbles. Nor did he neglect to mention, in these afternoon stories, the various mortifications that had beset him, the trouble he was having and the trouble he anticipated. That seemed to please his mother most of all, for she regarded him with a certain happiness, as though she were amused to be of still further use in his life.

Usually he had something to say about Peg, but instead of sympathy he met a baffling indifference. He would mention Peg and glower to indicate his infuriation. He was always surprised when his mother inevitably replied that she was sure Peg was a very nice boy.

"He's not," he said, quickly. "He's Limpy's

brother," which was to his mind explanation enough, for Limpy stayed in the streets all day and sometimes could be seen in alleys behind saloons. The fact that Peg was not Limpy's brother did not occur to him; he had simply stated what he believed ought to be true, for Limpy was the concern of the town, a villain acknowledged, and more than once Mark had been warned never to play with him. Besides, Limpy limped and Peg had broken a leg; surely they must be somehow related.

"Peg's not a good boy. *I* am . . . I am and Peg ain't!" Mark paused, for he saw one small ray of quality in Peg. "But he once broke his leg." Mark would give him that credit.

"Don't say *ain't*—say *isn't* . . . *is not*. A fine scholar, you are.

"Now run right upstairs and change your clothes."

"Well," said Mark, to clench his point, "I don't like him."

"Then that's your fault and you should *try* to like him."

"Like *him!*" That was inconceivable. "Besides, he don't like me—and I don't think he will try to, either." And he sighed, for he knew it was so. Turning away thoughtfully, he started toward the stairs.

That scene remained in his mind, clear-cut as a cameo, because suddenly his mother was very nice to him. She was in the kitchen; a dish towel was wrapped around her head, and her sleeves were rolled to her elbows. She had been polishing the silver, but when he started for the stairs, she called him back. She dried her hands and held him off at arm's length. "Let me look at you," she said; she brushed his hair back from his forehead. "I almost forgot what you look like, you've been gone so long," she said.

"All day," he said, with an expansive gesture.

"All day," she repeated, in his tone. "Think of that!"

Mark thought of it. It was rather wonderful.

"I wonder," he heard her saying, "if small boys grow very much in one day." He rather imagined they did. "You know what we'll do," she said, "we'll get some more film for the camera. I should send a picture to your father."

"In my school clothes?"

Yes, that's what she meant. As a rule, he disliked standing for pictures because the sun got in his eyes; and it meant standing still for a long time, but if he wore his school clothes, that would make a difference. He would hold a school book in front of him, so it would get in the picture, too. But he hadn't been given a book yet! That was a problem. He sat down in the chair, by the stove, to think about it.

Mark was not disappointed that despite his schooling he had not yet been taught how to read and write, but if he just had a book, just one book, he could carry it home from school, as the older fellows did. To be quite truthful, he was more interested in having a book than he was in learning his letters. Oh, it would be nice to be able to read the book. He had seen people reading; it was some place that they went without moving from their chair. They sat in their houses, intent in their books; and they read on the porches that he passed, with a newspaper in front of their faces; but he had no envy for them.

Adults imagine that children like to understand what they mean when, in hoarse tones, they spell out to each other their shocking messages. Still, Mark seemed to care little of what they were so laboriously telling each other. What he wanted was a school book, and he would like to have it right now, to have his picture taken with it. Well, it didn't look as though he was going to get it. Miss Matthews kept saying pretty soon.

Mark arose from his reverie and looked idly across the room at his mother. He saw her put polish on the rag and begin to rub briskly. "What're you doing?" he asked.

A fork was on a dish cloth, held between her knees, and she was scrubbing at it. It seemed to be difficult. "What are you doing?" he repeated. "Scrubbing the fork?"

She did not answer. Her chin must have been itching, for she was trying to rub it with her shoulder and polish the fork at the same time. "Mom," he said, "what are you *doing?* Are you busy *working?*" He was insistent, but his tone was very polite.

"Oh," she said, and looked up at him. "Well, you'll just have to forgive me, Mrs. Blodgett. This is the maid's day off today. But sit down—sit down, Mrs. Blodgett, and take your enormous weight off your feet."

He only partly understood what she meant, but this was the kind of talk he liked. It was the manner to be used for playing games, such as the Grocer Game, when he played the Grocer and asked the Housewife what he could do for her today. Sometimes, in fact, for long stretches of conversation at a time, he never knew what she was talking about; and when he interrupted the game to enquire, she would tell him that if he didn't look out he would grow up to be as intent as a minister's wife, so that there were times when he looked closely at Mrs. Rolphe, who was a minister's wife, to wonder what was so intent about her. It may have been because she had a big face.

That had led to a story. He had asked his mother if she would like to be a minister's wife, and she had replied she would have to take the question under consideration. Then he had enquired if she would like to be a grocer's wife. Yes, she would, if he carried fresh vegetables, too. Well, would she like to be a schoolteacher's wife—Mr. Blake's wife?

But the game ended there because she did not answer his question. "Would you?" he repeated, but the game was over, for then, in a different tone, she asked him if he saw Mr. Blake much at school. Did Mr. Blake talk to him, and what did Mr. Blake say?

Mark couldn't remember. He got up from his chair and gave a hop. "I'd like to play something," he said. He gave another hop and bumped into the table.

"All right," she said, "you play a small boy who has to go upstairs and change his clothes. You play that you have to do that right away . . . This room is a penitentiary, pretend, and you have to get out of it."

Mark sat down again, disappointed. "I don't want to play *that*—a *pen* what?"

"A pen-i-ten-tiary . . . But don't look so glum. I'm not really so anxious to get rid of you again."

"Then tell me a story!" But she said that she didn't know a story; he asked her if she would read him a story, then.

"You see I'm polishing the silver," she told him. He wished, then, that if she did not read him a story now, she would read him one after supper.

She thought for a moment. "As a matter of fact," she began, "I think I know a story . . ."

"A story about the penitentiary?" he asked, having almost overwhelming difficulty with the word.

"In that case," she said, "let's call it a castle instead."

That was good. He knew about castles. They

were stone walls with armor, with moats that had water in them; and once you were in a castle, you couldn't always get out. You couldn't always get in, for that matter; either the knights lowered the drawbridge or you had to have a siege. All castles had drawbridges, and horses could ride over them. His mother had written him a poem about that.

"Did the castle have a lady fair?" he asked, interested.

"Yes, she was fair enough."

"Did she live in the castle? Was that her home?"

He watched his mother closely, waiting for her answer. "No, hardly," she said. "You see, she was driven there. She was a captive . . . Oh, that's a good name for the story," she exclaimed, "The Captive in the Castle!"

He liked that title, too. "Who rescued her?" he enquired.

His mother paused and regarded him for a moment. "Well," she said, and smiled, "it wasn't a knight on a charger."

Not a knight? Who, then?

"Now, Mark, don't get so excited. Stories are supposed to rest you . . . This is a very resting story. It all began at a teaparty, and a very quiet teaparty, it was, not nearly as famous a one as Alice had with the Mad Hatter. You remember that one. Well, this afternoon the lady fair was very happy; she was happy because she was wearing a smooth, long gown that her mother had bought for her a week before in the city . . . And there's no need at all for excitement because, as I said, it was a very calm party, with everyone moving slowly to the murmur of extraordinarily polite conversation. There wasn't even a Dormouse to rattle a teacup, and the Lady Fair felt very cool and superior, in a contemplative sort of way, as she looked around and noticed that all the other lady fairs were wearing such stuff as fluffy organdie, in perfect comparison to the superiority of her voile."

Voile, teaparty, perfectcomparison? What did they mean? Mark had been listening carefully, but that failed to help. Where was the castle? "Mom," he said, "what does it mean?"

"What does what mean?"

"The story mean?"

"Come, Mark. I've told you before that you shouldn't have to be told what stories mean. Just listen, and you will understand them, or you will learn to. I don't want to confuse you, but I wouldn't want to be the kind of mother who feels she must stoop to talk to her child . . . You wouldn't want me to do that, would you—to *baby* you?"

"No, but . . ."

"It's the way we grow up," she continued—"by listening. That's the way our minds grow, just as our bodies grow by eating what we are told to eat. It's all right to ask questions, but stories shouldn't need questions. You remember the stories and pretty soon the questions answer themselves. That way we never forget them."

Mark now was as interested in this explanation as he was in the story. He leaned forward like a patient listening to his physician.

"You see," his mother said, "each of us has a memory, just as we have a body; and our memory works for us. That is how we remember to spell our name, or to find our way home, because our memory tells us how. Isn't that true?"

Yes, that was a story that Mark knew well. He nodded his head rapidly, in an alert manner, to reveal that he did indeed understand. "It's—like my heart!" he shouted.

"Well, not exactly. I'm afraid you are thinking of another story . . . One's heart is a crueler kind of compensation." She spread out the silver on the table. "No, you're too restless and excited for a story today. I'll tell it to you some other time. We'll call it 'The Captive in the Castle,' and we'll keep it in reserve—for when we need a story."

But it now became imperative that he hear the rest of it. He sat straight in his chair, anxious to meet approval. "The Lady Fair was in the Castle," he began, and waited as quietly as he could.

His mother changed her tone. She said that she had not meant to confuse him. "You are all ears today," she said. "But the Lady Fair wasn't in the Castle yet. However, we'll begin from there, and just ignore how she got there . . . The Lady Fair, then, was in the Castle, and the Knight . . ."

Mark forgot; he interrupted. "But you said there wasn't a Knight!"

"Did I? Well, he was, at that . . . but he was a different kind of knight. He was a kindly knight. He—he wore spectacles."

"Did he have a horse?"

"No, he didn't even have a horse."

That was a strange kind of knight. "Well, how did he rescue her then?"

"I'm coming to that. Let's see . . . he noticed her through a window. Yes, in a window, where she stood hard at work being pensive and woebegone, in a dazzling sort of way. And he came to her and said, 'Why do you live in this Castle, when you don't like anyone who lives here?' And he reminded her that the walls were of stone, very hard stone, too, it was; and that the air was gray . . . Besides, it was a very small Castle.

"This Knight went peering around in his spectacles for weeks at a time, weighing this and weighing that, and one day he came to the Lady Fair and said, 'This Castle isn't all that it seems to be.'

"She was very surprised. She lifted her eyebrows. See, like this, to show that she was surprised. 'No?' she said. 'No,' he replied, 'it's not only depressing, but it's very flimsy besides.'

"Then the Lady Fair told him, but she told him

- 49 -

as gently as she could, that she didn't think he could push it over with one hand.

" 'Perhaps not,' the Knight said, 'nor even with two hands. But this Castle is a product of the time. It only seems formidable from the inside. From the outside it's small and rather trivial—and I must say I imagine it's rather dull.'

"Again the Lady Fair was surprised, for she thought that at the very least her Castle was an interesting one.

" 'I can't even grant you that,' he said. 'It's just a morbid place to be. Yes,' he repeated, frowning at her over his spectacles, 'it's a morbid place to be. And you forget,' he added, 'that the Castle has a drawbridge. But maybe,' he said, and he looked at her shrewdly, 'you're the kind of Lady Fair that can't find the drawbridge for herself. Maybe you have to be *led* out.'

"The Lady Fair said very quickly, and very haughtily, too, for she was a sulky girl, that she could very well find her way out.

" 'Then you must like it here,' the Knight said, and with that he left. But he didn't go far. He came back every day and talked to his Lady Fair. He told her that people have very short memories, which was untrue; and he told her what people might think did not matter so much if you were not afraid of them—which was true. And she believed him, everything that he said."

His mother paused. She looked at him and smiled.

"And one day," she said, "he came to her and she was glad to let him lead her from the Castle."

"By the drawbridge?" Mark suggested. Yes, she told him, by the drawbridge. He frowned. "Did they just *walk* out?"

"Oh, no . . . You see, they saw a Dragon . . . They had to fight a Dragon. They were on their way out and they met this Dragon, and he was a very large dragon, with nineteen heads and twenty-two tails; but he couldn't hurt them at all, no matter how much he stamped around and snorted fire through his nostrils; no, no matter how angry he was, he couldn't do a thing to them. He could wave his tails and shake his many arms, but he was powerless to touch them, for he had only one eye, you see, and the Knight knew this, so he looked that Dragon right in the eye. Indeed, he looked at him so directly, and looked so hard, that the big Dragon just couldn't think of a thing to do except flinch. So he flinched; he flinched and he flinched, and the strain was so mighty that the drawbridge creaked and the abandoned Castle rocked to and fro, and the water in the moat became so unruly that the little fish had to swim upside down to keep their balance. But the Knight wasn't afraid. He took his Lady Fair by the hand—like this—and, still keeping his stare on the Dragon, walked right past him, over the pitching drawbridge and beyond the gates, to the forest . . . He took her to the safety and obscurity of the forest."

"Oh!" Mark exclaimed, and thought of his own forest, "to the forest to be his wedded wife!"

"Yes, to be his wedded wife."

Mark sighed. He could see them on the drawbridge. "And what happened to the Dragon?"

"He stayed on in the castle, roaming around from room to room, trying to forget his chagrin."

It seemed to Mark that somebody should have killed the Dragon. "I'd have done it," he said. "I'd have taken my broadsword and chop, chop, chop—chopped all his heads off!" And he made the threatening motions, to show his mother how easily he would have done it. He sank back in the chair and took a deep breath.

"Where'd they go—what happened to the Knight after that?" he asked.

"But that's all the story," his mother said.

"But don't you know where they went?"

"Oh, the Knight went away. He left the forest and went away—to the wars."

"For his Lady Fair?"

His mother shook her head. He thought for a moment. "Then why'd he go?"

"His King made him go. You see, he was a Knight and he did have a King."

"Did he win the wars?"

"No-oo."

"Did he lose?" No, he didn't lose either. "You forget," she told him, "that he was a very special kind of knight."

Mark didn't understand at all, but he knew he should not say so. "Did he kill anyone then?" he asked.

"Of course not," she said. "Where do you get all this killing on your mind?"

Mark could not see a good ending for this story. "Well, what did he do when he came back?"

"I don't know . . . It's just a story. He—he came back covered with medals, I guess."

Medals, that was good. "Don't you know for sure?"

"Come now, Mark," she said, "the story's over. They lived happily together for ever and ever—now why don't you let me finish the silver?"

"And was she there—his Lady Fair?"

"Yes, and you're a poet and don't know it . . . And you prattle; you're a prattler and a poet," she told him. She picked up a handful of knives and held them to the light.

In a moment she looked at him and laughed. She said he looked so serious. Deep in thought, he scarcely heard her. The afternoon sun came in the window, strong and broad, and tilted. It caught his attention, for he saw it looked like a drawbridge. Only it wasn't as long as it should be; it was blockier.

"Did you know," he said, after a long pause, "that we've blocks at school?"

"Real ones?"

"Yep, and they've got letters. The letters are in red and blue; we learn to spell by the letters."

"That's the way you learned to spell your name," she reminded him. "Do you spell your name with them—the ones at school?"

No, he did not; and that was a disappointment. But he let his mother reassure him that he would get a chance some day, just like pretty soon he would have a book. "You can't expect everything at once," she told him.

Mark was becoming restless. He had been sitting still for quite a long while. He stood up and tried to balance himself, with his feet off the ground, by holding on to the table. "Mother," he said; and when she failed to look up from her work, he said it again.

"Yes."

"I'm hungry."

"Don't worry, supper's coming. Just as soon as I finish the silver."

"But I'm hungry now," he explained.

"You can wait . . . You wouldn't want to eat with a rusty spoon, would you? Besides, you still have on your school clothes. Why don't you go right up and change now?"

He started toward the stairs, thinking about hunger. What did they eat in the Castle, and what did dragons eat? Human beings? What did they have at the teaparty, where ladies wore long dresses? All ladies wore long dresses, but girls didn't—but babies did, boy babies as well as girl babies, they all had to wear them.

Mark stopped on the stairs and looked down to his mother. He could see only her shoes, with the bottom of her dress around them. "Mother!" he called, "did that story happen once upon a time, a long time ago?"

"Yes," she replied. "Yes, it certainly did."

"How old was she—the Lady Fair?" About sixteen, she said she guessed.

"Well, how old would the Lady Fair be now?"

There was no answer for a moment; then he could see his mother bending over, almost to her knees, looking up at him. "What questions you ask," she said. "There's just no getting you upstairs."

"Well, how old would she be?"

"She would be about twenty-five, I think."

"Oh."

"*Oh*, what?"

"Oh, thank you, Mother," he said, correcting himself, saying thank you as he had been taught to say it. But it was not what she meant, he found, because she said, "Not at all. I didn't mean that. I should thank you."

But instead of really thanking him, she waved for him to go on—go on upstairs.

That's not as good a story, he thought, as the one with the deer than ran by day in the wooded glen, not nearly as good a story. Not as good, either, as the one of the boy Jack, the giant, and the beanstalk. He imagined that if he had his choice, he would choose for his favorite the one with the beanstalk. He had a picture of that, in a book his Aunt Carol gave him.

Anyway, he had to change his clothes. Once he was started, he did not mind dressing and undressing; it was just the getting started that was hard. There was a time when the whole thing was a monstrous task, with buttons that refused to button, stockings that had heels where toes should have been, and a baffling identity between the front and back of trousers; and there was a time when his mother or father had to help him. One thing yet, though, that he could not always do: he couldn't buckle his shoe. On the other hand, that was nothing to be ashamed of, even though Richard did know how to do it. After all, as he told Richard, clothing was one thing and shoes were another. Having his shoe buckled for him did not at all detract from his complete ability to change his own clothes.

As a matter of fact, he had not been allowed his own room until he had thus proven himself able to keep care of his person. His room was a fine one. It had a picture in it and the name of the picture was "The Lone Wolf"; he was very proud of it, indeed. It was the only one in the house that he truly liked. He did not care for those in his mother's room. Some were called "pastels" and they were soft and fuzzy. There were two others, less fuzzy, but equally disagreeable. One was "Cupid Awake" and the other was "Cupid Asleep"; and one was as bad as the other. He never bothered to understand why he disliked them, but it must have been because Cupid was plump and pink, and singularly lacking in biceps. Another picture, over by the closet, was of a baby, a real one, not a grown-up baby like Cupid. When you looked at this picture, you surprised the baby in bed, playing with his toe. And the baby, too, was plump and pink. Mark's father was plump, people said, but he was large, and he wore spectacles; that made a difference. But babies, Mark considered them to be like little frogs, and not at all related to him.

His father's office was directly below his own room, but he was not allowed to enter it. Once, when he did, a man was in there, sitting on the table, with his shirt off; his father had that stethoscope against the man. He remained very quiet, this scene was so fascinating, but without even turning around to see if he was there, his father said, "Mark, your mother's calling you." But when he left to see what she wished, she said that she hadn't called him at all. Now he couldn't even go in the room at any time. It was almost as if that room were a house of its own; it even had its own doorway and a path to the gate. He could see who went in, and he could watch them when they came out; but he never was able to see them in that room.

He could go into the other six rooms, though. And Mark knew every piece of furniture and every picture in all of them. What with rainy days and the chicken pox, he had been confined so often to the house that many of the things in it became personified. There was a large leather chair in the sitting room, with a smoking stand beside it. The chair had a name. He was Grandfather, and the smoking stand was called Happy. Grandfather and Happy once fought the Indians together, but now they sat side by side in the corner of the front room and in low tones talked of the good old days.

The room was panelled in dark wood and led into the dining room, where there was a fumed oak table, with chairs to match the table and the panelling. The whole room, upon the right occasion, became a railroad roundhouse, so that sometimes trains went around and around, all day long, under the table.

The dining room had two pictures, one of a bowl of flowers and the other of a basket of implausible apples. Below the height of the pictures, a panel ledge ran around the room; upon it were miniature boys and girls, cats and dogs, and seashells like tiny plates. There was a time when he was not supposed to touch them, but sometimes he would forget, for by climbing up on a chair he could just barely reach the little boys and girls; but whenever he touched them, they fell down, and once in a while one would fall clear to the floor and, bang! it would break. Later, however, he was encouraged to play with these on rainy days, and he did play with them once or twice; but his heart wasn't in it.

Of all the rooms, though, Mark preferred his

own, not only because he lived there, but also because he could draw down the window shade so far that the window itself became a peephole, just wide enough for him to aim his wooden rifle through, but not large enough for an arrow to slip in and catch him unawares. Then, too, his windowsill could be employed as the foundation for a hoist. He kept a rope in his room, to be used whenever he found any old nails or rusty pieces of iron; these he would tie loosely to one end of the rope and lower that end, with its burden, down the wall of the house to some hydrangea bushes on the ground below. Then he shook the rope until the iron fell out; if he was lucky, it fell beneath the bushes. The iron turned the blue flowers to pink. Mark was glad to cooperate with them; he felt that he was doing something rather valuable.

Yes, it was good to have a room of one's own; and when he looked from his window, he did not necessarily have to see the domestic roses that surrounded that side of the house. He could look higher, past the bent apple tree, and on to the pines; and if he looked hard enough, there could occasionally be seen a dark figure prowling in between the trunks.

But today he was not searching for bad men. He was preoccupied with thoughts of the story, and his room, and his life of frustration at school. As he at last got into his overalls, he decided that tomorrow for sure he would spell his name in letters. And if Peg were present, he would dare him to do the same. Maybe, when Miss Matthews saw that he was unable to spell his own name, she would spank his hands with the fly-swatter; and when, in terror, Peg ran away, he would fall over the blocks and break his leg again. How he would laugh at that fellow!

Mark would have gloated further over the catastrophe he foresaw for Peg, but he heard his mother call from downstairs; he left behind him all thoughts of vengeance as he ran, with his shoes loose, half-tripping, down the stairs. He meant to ask his mother if he would be able to spell or if he would have some school books by the time his father came home, but he tripped on the last step and, with a wild Indian whoop, came skidding into the kitchen. He sat down heavily and lifted his foot. "Fix my shoe, please," he said.

"But you've changed into your overalls," his mother said. "I meant for you to put on your nightgown and robe . . . You will have to go right to bed after supper."

"Right after supper?"

"Yes, you do. You don't get your afternoon naps anymore."

He was still frowning. "But *right* after supper," he said, as though all the world were against him.

But she was determined. "You just have to, that's all. Don't worry, I want you there no more than you want to be there, or any sooner, either . . . Now let's see your shoe."

He lifted up his foot again and his mother bent down. She had a little difficulty, for the room was getting dark. Outside the last of the sun was leaving, and as it left the pine trees came closer. He could just see the things on the table. His mother fixed one shoe, and lifted up the other. His father did it better. His father's hands moved quickly and surely; he could do tricks with them, too. He would put a nickel in his hand and wink his eye, then the nickel would be gone.

"Did you have a letter from Daddy today?" he asked.

"No," she said.

She returned to the pantry and brought him a glass of milk; and alongside his plate she put an apple. He drank almost half the milk without stopping, and put down the glass with a gesture. That's the way a man did it.

"Mother," he asked, "were you ever sixteen, like a Lady Fair?"

He looked across the table at her; she had her hand on her chin and was looking at him, without seeming to see him, as though she were tired. "Were you—were you ever sixteen?"

"No," she replied, "never."

He was happy to hear that. It was true that for days he scarcely thought about her, but when he did, he remembered her as she was now, for he could scarcely imagine that she had ever been anything except his mother.

Fourth Chapter

THERE WAS only one trouble with having your house on the edge of the forest. No other houses could be near. Almost everyone seemed to live away from you, down in the town below, so that it was only by special arrangement that you could play with the fellows at all.

There was but one house close to Mark's place; it was the house where a small girl lived. She was Mr. Blake's daughter, Judith. Somehow her place had not been on the hill as long as his house, because people spoke of the new Blake place and the old Blake place; the old place was much larger and it was way down the hill, deep in the town, and no one lived in it anymore. But as long as Mark could remember, people spoke of the Douglases and the Blakes, and the Blakes and the Douglases, as though the two went together. People asked him about Judith as much as they asked him of his father and mother, and he always replied that she was all right, he guessed, because he disliked to be asked that question.

After all, Judith was a girl; there was no escaping that fact, and that in itself was the cause of much trouble, for already Judith had developed the maternal inclination to keep care of people. His mother said that Judith realized her feminine responsibility; she knew that Mark needed her attention. Judith felt that she and his mother were doing wonders for him.

Judith enjoyed lengthy talks with his mother about him, and in their presence he found in himself a certain uneasiness. For one thing, Judith made it plain that she was his for sympathy, had he wanted it, and it was a source of annoyance to her that he did not. When he turned away from her, she would go sit down and, as though she were alone, begin moving her lips, talking to herself in a kind of dream.

She was older than he was; six months older, as she often reminded him, and that was half a year; in matters of opinion she was reasonably confident that she knew best. "But Mark," she would say, "you must do what I say. I'm older than you and I know what's best for you." And sometimes she would act as if he had no mind of his own, as though he could be addressed only through a third person. "Oh," she would say, "I love Mark! I love Mark, Mrs. Douglas. He's a nice boy." She would say that and try to put her arms around his shoulders, but she would be looking at his mother instead of at him. Once he hit her in the eye and had to go sit in the closet.

Yet, even though Judith was indeed the inevitable young girl who likes to play mother, she came very close in appearance to the blue-eyed and golden-haired princesses in the fairy stories; only in spirit was she Judith. Her hair shone fine in the light and, if her mother helped it a little, came by itself into curls; her features were fragile, yet often strength came into them, and no matter how she felt, even if she was as tired as he was, she always acted very polite. In fact, as everyone said, and the boy seemed to suspect, Judith was too good to be true.

She was slight, though, and usually ailed of one thing or another; still her ailments belonged to the nineteenth century and were vague and concealed, really a trifle mysterious, rather than anything as plain and ordinary as measles. Indeed, it would have been impossible to associate such a disease with Judith. Other girls might catch their cases outright, and make much of them, but germs with Judith were more subtle.

No, Judith was not as others were, unfortunately for everyone. Parents said how sweet she was and that she was such a fine example, so that in younger eyes she often was watched with suspicion. Her arms and legs were very thin and people said she was delicate, but she never had an awkward age, and she never giggled. There was that much Mark could say for her, but of course he never did.

Naturally it was Judith who won the Gold Star. She came home with it pasted on her report card at the end of the school's first quarter. The afternoon was a memorable one to Mark, too, but for a different reason. On his way home from school he passed the railroad station and saw a crowd there; it was a strangely exciting sight, for soldiers were there by the railroad train, two of them, with rifles held at their shoulders. They were standing beside a long box that had an American flag spread over it, and a lot of people from the town were there. But there were even more people near the other end of the train, waving and calling to some soldiers who were being helped down the steps. These soldiers had those little brown hats that looked like brown paper-sailboats. He noticed that one of the soldiers was using a crutch and that two men were guiding another soldier into a farm wagon. He began to comprehend, with a tingling of excitement, why so many people were at the station, and when he finally realized, he began running home as fast as he could to tell his mother about it.

"Wounded soldiers, wounded soldiers!" he shouted as soon as he reached the door. Real soldiers, he thought—real wounded soldiers! They had been shot by guns! Mark shivered with excitement. His mind seemed to be saying it, over and over again—Bang, Bang, as though he were playing with a cap pistol.

But his mother already knew. He found her in the front room, selecting some books; and he noticed that she had placed some jars of jelly and fruit on the dining room table. He wanted to know what she was doing.

"I'm going over to Mrs. Barnes' in an hour or so," she replied. "You can stay at Judith's until I return for dinner."

"Are you going to give her the books?" he asked, opening one to see if it had any pictures.

"I'm taking them over there for her boy," she told him.

Mark knew Mrs. Barnes because she sometimes helped Mr. Blair at the Confectionary, but he did not know she had a little boy. "Not a little boy," his mother said. She hesitated, "You remember Johnny Barnes . . . he came home today. He went to war—and he came home today sick.

"That's why I'm bringing the fruit," she added.

Mark wanted to know if he had influenza. "No, he's just sick," she told him. Mark closed the book with a bang and gave a hop. Tonight, he decided, he would help Mr. Blake in the garden. He wondered if Mr. Blake had ever been a soldier, like this soldier who was sick.

"Did he fight the Germans?" he asked. She evidently did not hear him. "Did he fight them—the one who's sick?"

"He used to be the grocer's boy," his mother said. "You know him. The day before he left, he came up and said good-bye."

Now, as soon as she said it, Mark knew who Johnny Barnes was. He drove the grocery cart and the horse had white feet, but he wouldn't give Mark a ride because sometimes, he said, the horse shied at automobiles . . . Why Johnny Barnes was the one they talked about at school! At first Mark had not understood what they meant . . . He turned to his mother.

"Do you mean the one," he asked, "who had his legs shot off?"

As soon as he said it, Mark realized that something had happened to his mother. She acted as though this had happened, and she would not hear him. "They said he had his legs shot off," he told her; but even as he watched, the book she had taken from the shelf, slid from her hand and fell, split open, on the floor.

Mark looked down at the book and then at his mother. Something had happened, but he had seen nothing happen. "What's the matter, Mother?" he asked anxiously, for now he feared that what he had said was bad.

She spoke to him quietly; she wanted to know who had told him that. "I'm not fibbing," he said, "honest, I'm not."

"Who told you?" she asked him, again, as though she were angry at him.

"At school," he replied, almost whining. "They told me at school, honest." He had said one of those things that he should not say; he would be warned growing boys don't say those things. "I'm not fibbing," he told her again, "they said it at school lots of times, a long time ago."

Almost in terror, for he was frightened most by things that he could not understand, he stooped and picked up the book. He held it out to her at arm's length.

"Do you think I am going to hit you?" she asked.

"No."

"Have I ever hit you?"

No, but—he did not know what was wrong. Almost before he thought of it, he ran to her; and as soon as she put her arms around him, he knew that whatever was wrong, was almost all right now. "Mark," she began, tentatively; and paused. "That is not something for a boy to remember." He was afraid of that slow and evasive tone she was using; he pressed his head harder against her shoulder, for her to pay attention to him instead of what she was saying. But she lifted him away from her and looked at him kindly.

"Now," she said, "now, now, what's the matter? No one's going to hurt you . . . It's simply that you must not think about Johnny's sickness any more.

You mustn't think of it at all. It's all over now and we won't talk about it anymore."

"But it's what happened, isn't it? Didn't he really?" Why did she call it sickness? He had to know.

"I just finished telling you," she said, "that you must not talk about it." Now she was not as kind to him as she had been before. She walked into the dining room and put the book with the other things on the table. He had his legs shot off, he had his legs shot off, Mark said in his mind. He knew it was bad to say it, but there was something in the words that fascinated him, and he repeated them until they ran together in a rhythm, even after he had forgotten they were moving in his mind.

This was not the first time that his mother had been angry when he told her of things he heard at school. He was learning that he should not tell her everything he heard; he should not always run to her, not that he knew why, exactly; it was just that sometimes he said things that were wrong, although they were not wrong until he said them to his mother. But he could not help imagining what a soldier would look like that way. Limpy had a crooked leg, as bent as a bough of the old witch's tree, and Peg had once broken a leg. Mark wondered if anything would happen to his legs. It must hurt a great deal, he imagined, to have something wrong like that. He wondered idly, as he wearied of the subject, if there was some way that they could grow back.

Life was becoming complicated. In his own world there was seldom confusion, but that much of the adult world which filtered into his mind was almost beyond comprehension. His mother was shocked that he knew the tragedy that came to Johnny Barnes, in this adult undertaking of war, but she had mistaken his curiosity for horror; she intended to protect him from this pain and tragedy of her own world, for she could not realize that he had no precedent in his feelings for either pain or tragedy. Instead he had a curiosity, and that curiosity satisfied itself only in his thrilled fascination, that clung to the new, the extraordinary, and the horrible.

At Judith's house, where he had gone to await his mother's return, he listened with little interest to her extravagant statements about the Gold Star. It was, it seemed, a mark of utmost importance.

"You see," Judith explained, attempting to stand on her toes, and therefore swaying dizzily, "you see, it's my reward for Endeavor—just like it says." She handed the card to Mark that he could see for himself. "It's the very highest honor," she said. And there it was, pasted to the top of her report card, in all its tinsel splendor. "And it's the only gold star in the room," she added, glancing modestly at her mother.

Mrs. Blake took the card from Mark. To him she scarcely had an identity. She was a hand that gave him something or took something away, and she was a mouth that spoke words. Whenever he thought of her, and that was only when her name was mentioned, he did not recall her by her face or manner. He recalled an apron, with a dress behind it, and a flat voice that talked endlessly about Judith, from a face that was gray and oval, but somehow too vague for recollection. Even when he was in her home, he never looked at her; or if he did, she made no impression in his mind. He realized she was there, and that she was talking, but for him she remained a presence rather than a person.

Mrs. Blake was reading aloud Judith's report card. "She got a *1*," she told him, "in everything except Music."

Judith interrupted to say that she did not seem to be very proficient in Music. "But I haven't been late to school once; and I got all my answers right —and Miss Matthews says I know all my lessons . . . She says I must keep up the good work!"

"Well, I'm proud of you, Dear," Mark heard Mrs. Blake say, "and your father will be delighted —unless he knows already!"

Judith danced up and down, and flung her arms around in a circle. "Maybe he'll let me have the kitten now!" she cried, breathlessly; but the spinning had made her dizzy, and she slid forward into a chair.

"She has a music of her own ringing in her ears," Mrs. Blake said to Mark, who did not at all know what she meant.

Judith jumped up and grabbed his hand. "Let's play school!" she shouted. He replied that he did not care to. "Come on," she said, "I'll be teacher," but Mark still shook his head. He looked around the room, hunting for something he could do by himself.

"Do you want to play dolls, then?" she asked, after a moment. Mark did not. "Don't you want to play dolls?" she repeated, in great surprise.

"No!" he said, and gave her a glare.

Judith turned to her mother in exasperation. "He won't play," she complained. Mark stared at her and then at Mrs. Blake's apron. Just let them try to make him do anything.

"Make him play school," Judith said. "I want to play Teacher." Mark shook his head. "He won't do anything!" Judith said, and stamped her foot. Mrs. Blake shrugged her shoulders. "You can lead a horse to water," she said, and smiled at Judith, who frowned.

"You can lead a horse to water . . ." her mother repeated, as though she were nudging her. Judith laughed and Mrs. Blake laughed. It was the same kind of laugh as a giggle and Mark felt uneasy.

"Well, he's a boy," he heard Mrs. Blake saying, "you go ahead and play without him.

"You can sit in here and look at the books, if you

want, Mark," she added, and returned to the kitchen.

Judith flung herself into a chair and Mark sat down across the room, watching her idly. She returned the look, so after a moment he turned away and reached for a book. He wanted that book with the bright blue cover, the one that had horses in the front of it, then wagons and trains, a dog-sled, and later, automobiles. It was the book that he liked best at Judith's house. He held up the book. "Look at the automobiles," he said, but Judith wrinkled up her nose at him. "Come look at the horses, too," he urged her. She made a face again, so he put his free hand to his ear and wiggled it at her. She stuck out her tongue. "Huh!" he replied, in disgust, and put the book down, and used both hands to make fun of her. She turned abruptly, swinging her legs to the arm of the chair. He wiggled his fingers some more, but she could not see him; he returned his attention to the book.

No more than a few moments had passed since he came to her house, but his time usually moved in such slow motion that it seemed to him that he must have been here almost an hour, and an hour, he knew, was almost an age. He sighed and flipped the pages. He wished he had a horse to go galloping over the country, up one mountain and down another, the hooves moving up and down with a clatter, while he hung on carelessly with one hand and swung his great hat with the other.

"Whoaa!" he cried, "bang, bang, bang!" He glanced up at Judith, thinking he might take aim to shoot her, but she was still looking the other way, sullenly watching her foot as it swung to and fro.

In a moment he heard Judith asking her mother if she could have tea, real tea, for Pacida. Mrs. Blake replied that hot water ought to do, but Judith became very excited. Mark could sense the tension in the moment.

"But the Gold Star," Judith said, and ran to her mother, who stood in the doorway of the kitchen. Mrs. Blake said that in this case, she could, to be sure, have a real tea for Pacida. But she murmured, as Mark had often heard her say, that she believed it was time that Judith was forgetting this Pacida and things like that.

Mark knew, though, that Judith still regarded Pacida as her closest friend, and he realized that she must, of course, have tea with her this important afternoon. As Judith remarked, giving Mark a significant look, this Pacida was the only child in the world who could completely appreciate the honor of the Gold Star. Whom could she tell, when no one lived near?

It was obvious, even to Mark, that Pacida was the person to tell. Pacida and her family lived near Judith's house, in a large vacant space behind the sandpile. They really didn't live, of course; Judith admitted that. It was simply that she could pretend that they were real. They existed in her mind and depended upon her imagination, but to Judith that made little difference. She knew the whole family. There was Mr. Jenson, the father; Mrs. Mamie Jenson, the mother; Tommy, who was four years old; and the Baby, who had no other name. Mark found that he confused Tommy with the Baby, a confusion which strangely irritated Judith, who had to straighten them out for him, over and over again, nearly every time she mentioned any of the Jensons.

Mark failed to understand that the Baby mattered much, anyway. The Baby slept, that was all. Pacida, the sister, was exactly Judith's age, going on eight years old. Judith had known the Jensons for some time, since she was four, in fact. She met them one day while she was playing in the sandpile; they were just suddenly there. (That was before the Baby was born.)

Mark often heard Judith talking to them. He tried to talk to them, but not only was his attempt a failure, but Judith was angry, besides. Pacida would call for tea and Judith would serve her; and, in those tentative days of first acquaintance, Judith's mother came in, at Judith's request, to say hello to Pacida.

Mr. Jenson himself never went anywhere. He simply sat in his rocking chair, on the front porch of his house in the large vacant space, reading his paper. Pacida's mother seemed to earn the family's living. She also sat, but her place was in a little house, no larger than a telephone booth, by the railroad track, where all day long she pasted wheels on the trains that went by. It was a wearisome, and, for the most part, a thankless task.

The consequence was that Pacida had to do all the housework, for she was the oldest daughter. She swept not only the entire house—and it was a dusty house—but she also had to sweep the porch, and sweep carefully, too, under Mr. Jenson's chair, for he would not even move aside for a minute.

Pacida pleaded with her father; it was no use.

"Please, Daddy, won't you move aside a little so your daughter can get the dust from under you?"

But he would not reply; that's the kind of a man he was.

"Father dear, this is your own Pacida asking you to move just a little bit," she would say, and her lovely blue eyes would be eager with anguish.

But no; Mr. Jenson might grunt, but that was all, except that there would be times when the air crackled with the angry rustle of newspaper pages rapidly turning. That would be Daddy in search of news.

Yes, it was a trying life for a young girl like Pacida. Judith was eager to help her all that she could; and she could, at least, bring her in for tea, for that took the weight off her feet. Judith, though, never went to the Jensons for tea; it was not in her heart to like Mr. Jenson.

This afternoon at tea was much like any other, except that by the time the water was boiling, both girls had a Gold Star. "I believe yours is the nicest," Pacida said to Judith; "Its points are brighter."

"Perhaps you are right," Judith replied, "but I like yours, too. Still, it is a pity that you could not have done better in Arithmetic."

"Well, the truth is, Judith, I am just not as smart as you are. You're the smartest girl I know."

"Yes, I guess I am, but I am sure that you are the second smartest. I am sure that Mark is way below you . . ." She paused, then repeated: "I think *Mark* is *way* below you. I think he's ornery, don't you? If I were his mother I'd just make him mind."

Mark looked up from his book to stare at Judith, but she wasn't even looking at him. She was enclosed in some kind of a circle, and he could not get in that circle, even though he wished to be there. It was sort of a private place, he realized, and yet it somehow seemed that Judith was using this private place unfairly.

He decided to ignore her, no matter what she said; he stalked, with dignity, into the front room, leaving them chattering over their tea. He stood by the front door in a solemn fashion, scarcely noticing what he saw, until, looking way down the street, he saw Mr. Blake coming.

"Your father's coming home from school!" he called to Judith, and then grabbed his cap and ran out to meet him. He was certainly glad to see Mr. Blake. Now they could work in the garden.

All that time he and Mr. Blake had to wait in the house while Judith and her mother talked about the

Gold Star seemed an eternity and a pity to Mark. Judith had started dancing up and down again.

"So," her father was saying, "so," as he read down the list. "Very good—very good, indeed. That's the way a card should be." He started to hang up his hat. He seemed less straight and tall with his hat off, as if he were softer and rounder.

"But the Gold Star!" Judith cried, running after her father.

"Yes, of course, the Gold Star. I'm proud of you. Here, give me a kiss," and he lifted her up and kissed her on the cheek.

Mark stood on one foot and then the other; he wanted to get out of the house and get started, but Mr. Blake was acting as though there was no hurry at all.

Mrs. Blake dried her hands on her apron and then helped her husband with his overcoat. "What do you think of our daughter?" she asked. "Isn't she pretty fine!"

"It's the only one in the room!" Judith explained, rushing the words together.

"Oh, is that so. Well, well." He looked at Mark. "I'll be right with you," he said.

"But Daddy," Judith began. "Now can I . . ."

Her father interrupted her. "Yes," he said, "I know just what you're going to ask, and the answer is yes. If it's all right with your mother, you may have the kitten."

Mark could see that was exactly what Judith

wanted him to say. The kittens belonged to Mr. Anderson, whose farm was nearby, on the side road. She had wanted a kitten ever since the day the litter was born; he could have had one a long time ago, but he wanted a dog. Judith couldn't have hers because her father had read in the paper of a man who died from a cat scratch.

"Can I go over to Mr. Anderson's now?" he heard Judith ask. She looked from her father to her mother. She would have to hurry.

"Certainly, you go right now, if you wish," Mr. Blake told her.

But Mrs. Blake said no. "I don't know that she should go this evening," she said. "Tomorrow."

"But Mama!"

"Now, Dear, there'll be plenty of time for the kitten. Besides, you can help your father clear the garden."

"Oh, let her go if she likes," Mr. Blake said. "We can handle the garden, can't we, Mark?"

"No, it's late . . . And you two don't have much time together, anyway," she replied.

Judith turned her back on all of them, and Mark felt sorry for her. He knew how she felt, that she was a long way from her kitten. Mr. Blake walked toward the back door and Mark started after him, but as he left he saw Mrs. Blake make a sign for Judith to follow them. "What's the matter," he heard her whisper, hoarsely, "don't you like to help your father?"

Out in the yard Mark helped Mr. Blake strip some dead branches from the rose bushes. The air was becoming cold enough that when he breathed, he had a slight mist around his mouth. He pretended it was smoke. He looked to see if Judith were smoking like this, too; but Judith was standing quietly on the hard ground, on the mud that the frost had frozen, hugging herself. "I'm cold," she said, "under here"—and she indicated her skirts. Mr. Blake told her to run into the house for a warmer coat.

When Judith reappeared, she brought Mark his coat. Mr. Blake helped him put it on. "Have you got your report card with you?" he asked Mark, but Mark had already given it to his mother. "Well, what kind of grades did you get?" Mr. Blake asked. Mark assured him that he had forgotten.

"Mark did fine," Judith said, giving him a warm look.

"No, let Mark tell me. . . . How did you do in spelling? Do you understand it?"

"I don't know," Mark replied, after a moment, which was his way of saying that certain words he had spelled were finally decided by Miss Matthews to be slightly incorrect. His answer, he felt, would be explanation enough.

But it was not enough for Mr. Blake. "You don't know!" he exclaimed. "Well, now that *is* strange."

Mark did not know what to say; he became intent patting down the earth around a dried tulip bulb that happened to be there. He took a stick and drew a circle around the bulb. Now, he thought, suddenly preoccupied, now if I had some water, this could be a moat and the bulb a castle. Indeed, he had become so quickly preoccupied with what he was doing that he scarcely heard what Mr. Blake said to him about the rose bush.

"The blooms," Mark heard him say, "will be white, and I shall have the bush photographed. I'll give you a copy," he added.

Judith asked if she could have a copy, too. "Surely," he said, "you can take it to Miss Matthews and show it to the class . . . That's a good idea, don't you think, Mark?"

Mark thought that would be fine, but it was not a new idea. Mr. Blake had been promising the pictures ever since he could remember. He knew all about the rose, too; Mr. Blake had given it a name. It was the Blake Rose.

Judith stepped up to the bush, to touch it in an awed fashion, but what she touched was a last season's thorn; she cried out and put her finger in her mouth.

"Here, here," Mr. Blake said, "ladies have to be careful of their hands. . . . Before you get to be a much older lady, I'll have to get you some garden gloves."

Judith jumped up and down, her finger still in her mouth. "White gloves—like yours?" she cried.

"Yes, for the thorns . . . I'll get you the same kind I got Mark."

Nothing more was said. Mark and Mr. Blake worked in silence and Judith stood nearby, smiling and trying to help them. Mark had raked quite a pile of old branches and dead leaves together when he heard his mother calling him to supper. He got up off his knees and brushed off his overalls.

"Good-bye," he said, in a hesitant manner, for he did not want to leave until the work was done.

"Good-bye," Mr. Blake replied, "you did a good job tonight."

That was exactly what Mark wanted to hear; and when he heard it, he felt warm all over.

Still, as he ran across the field, he felt that he had done something vaguely wrong. He had not fibbed, nor had he said anything wrong this time; but he did feel uneasy, and when he got into the warm house, he still wished that Mr. Blake out there had not asked him that question about his spelling.

Fifth Chapter

THAT EVENING Mark was not happy. He was not unhappy, nor was he happy, for there is a difference. There was a thought in his mind; and a thought is a very dominating thing. He failed to remember about Johnny Barnes or to ask his mother for a new story; it even escaped his notice that she was as preoccupied as he, and that supper had been eaten in almost a silence. She may have feared that he, too, had been depressed by the return of the war's first wounded, but that, in his memory, happened centuries ago and was pushed back to a distant position by the mighty concern he had this moment. When he was told to go to bed, he trudged upstairs to undress in a thoughtful and methodical fashion. Like Adam, who had himself partaken of Knowledge, Mark knew a shame.

This shame that bothered him was too much, he found, for him to hold, so that before he made his peace for the night he had to tell his mother that confidentially not only Mr. Blake but he, too, regretted that the Gold Star had gone to another.

"What gold star?" she asked.

Now it had to be told. "You know, *the* Gold Star," he replied, for he hoped that would be clear enough.

"But what gold star—a gold star for what?"

"Oh," he exclaimed, as if he were beginning to understand. "The Gold Star for getting lessons right in school."

"I didn't know there was such a thing."

"Yes—there is, all right," he told her in a reassuring tone. "They come on cards . . . You look on my report card and you won't find one. But that's where they come, on the cards." And he gazed at his mother in enquiry. Could he be of further service.

"Well," she said, looking down at him, "you're growing up, I guess; you're getting evasive . . . But why? Didn't you do your lessons well? Why, I thought your card was a good one."

Mark looked at her, but couldn't think of anything to say. "Who gets the Gold Star?" she asked him. "The first in the class?"

"Judith did," he told her.

"So," he heard her murmur thoughtfully. "And what did he say? I mean, what did Mr. Blake say about the Gold Star?"

It was hard for Mark to remember. "He said . . . ah . . . he said—it was too bad that I couldn't get one, too."

"Like Judith did, I suppose."

"Yes, Judith got it on her report card. . . . Miss Matthews said that maybe next time somebody else would get it, too. She said we all should try to get it. She said that next time it might be hard to tell who should get it. She said we were a wonderful class, and she said—she said . . . But that's all she said, Mom, really."

"Here, don't get so excited. It's your sleep time." She sat on the edge of the bed and put her hand on his shoulder. She squeezed his arm and laughed. She seemed cheerful; maybe she'd stay with him awhile.

"You must remember that Judith is your friend," she explained. "And so you want to be glad that your friend won the award. Aren't you glad?"

Yes, he guessed he was. But she was a girl.

"Then you must tell her tomorrow how glad you are . . .

"Because you know," she continued, "how proud I am of you. Well, he's just as proud of Judith as I am of you." She hesitated.

"Mark," she said, "you know, I think that if you would clear out those ramble bushes in the back yard that you could have a garden for yourself in the Spring. A garden of your very own! Wouldn't that be fun!"

For a moment Mark thought that it would be fun, and then he wasn't sure. He couldn't put it into words, but what he meant was the garden in itself was not as much fun as helping Mr. Blake with his work.

But his mother must have misunderstood him, for she assured him that he could invite Judith over to his place. She would help him with his garden—his *own* garden, she added.

But that was something else. "But I don't play with Judith. She's a girl." That was reason enough. No sir, he didn't play with girls. And that was a comforting thought. In fact, the more he thought about it, the more comfortable he became, for the bed had at first been cold; but it was getting warm now.

"When did all this begin—this not liking girls?" his mother asked.

Mark did not know; he just suddenly felt that way. Fellows didn't play with girls.

"Nonsense," she said. "Is that what you learn at school?"

"Fellows don't play with girls," he repeated, stubbornly. It was a fact. He was astounded that his mother did not know about it.

"Well," she said, "you would like to have your own garden, wouldn't you? Sure, you would." She tucked the covers around his shoulders. Mark was very comfortable now; he didn't care one way or the other.

"That's a good boy," she said, and leaned over and kissed him. Now she was going to leave.

"Mom, leave the door open." And he looked anxiously to see if she would.

She paused with her hand on the knob. "Don't you think you're getting too big a boy to have the hall light on?"

Mark considered the problem for a moment. Somehow it was not the kind of question one could answer with a yes or no. But, after a moment, he said, "No."

"Why, you're not afraid of anything. You're the bravest fellow I know. Aren't you?"

"Yes," Mark replied, thoughtfully, for he was none too sure of it.

"Then what would a brave boy like you be doing with a light on to go to sleep?"

"Just leave it on tonight, Mom." He was awake now, and becoming really anxious.

. "What would there be to hurt you?"

That was true. How did he know exactly what would be there to hurt him? He had no way of telling, and neither did his mother. He could speak of many things that he saw sometimes, things in the dark with cloaks on, that might wish to injure him. But he did not speak of them, for he was but partly convinced they existed. After all, he was the beginning of a man. Nothing frightened his father. Besides, he had spoken before of these dark things, many times before, and no one had put much belief in his statements.

In the look that Mark gave his mother, he hoped that he made it clear, without openly admitting it, that for the satisfaction of them both she should leave the hall light burning and the door open. She must know he would compromise upon only a slight opening, even though that allowed no more than a crack of light to enter. That was only reasonable. But she wasn't going to do it; he could see that. His mind raced for something to say to keep her in the room, if only for another moment.

"What were you saying about the garden?" he said, slowly.

"Nothing," his mother said. "Go to sleep."

"No, tell me, Mom——please."

But she refused to stay.

"Good night," she said, "positively!" She kissed him again. Then she left the room, closing the door behind her. Mark lay very quietly.

After a moment a pale light came into the bedroom from the window and spread across his bed. He noticed that the counterpane looked blue instead of white. That would be something to tell his mother! But even as he listened, her footsteps ended. She must be all the way down stairs. Then he knew that by leaving she had made a grave mistake.

Mark did not want to look toward the closet door; he tried to keep his eyes away from it and think of something else, but even as he thought about it——he looked. Eyes wide open, his breath held, he glanced sideways toward the closet, in a stealthy manner.

And there it was, sure enough! That black thing again!

He ducked down in the covers. *"Mother!"* he called, once, but loudly, and he did not look again.

His mother came into the room. "Well?" she said. She had loosened her hair and it lay across her shoulders.

Mark looked at once to the closet, but the big thing was gone! "There was a big thing standing over by the closet door," he explained.

His mother tightened her lips and walked over to the closet. "See," she said, "there's nothing here," and that was true.

Whether he was grateful or chagrined, Mark did not know; but in himself he knew a certain disappointment. Perhaps it would have been better for him had there been *something* there. Nothing very serious, of course, but just some little black thing that his mother could have seen for herself.

"You go back to sleep," she said, "and quit imagining things."

Now she was going to leave again. "Did you know," he began, "that when the moonlight's in my room, this part of the bed is blue and this part of the bed is gone?"

"Is *that* a fact?" she said.

"And did you know—no, I don't mean and-did-you-know. I mean—what did you say about Mr. and Mrs. Blake?"

"I didn't say anything about them."

Mark was being deliberate, dragging his words to take up time. "I mean, if I have a garden of my own, can I still help Mr. Blake?"

"If you wish—but I don't think it will be necessary."

"But he likes to talk to me, Mom. I help him a lot."

"I'm afraid he's a very busy man. You may just get in his way."

"But can I, Mom?"

"Listen," she said, and she was very firm, "it's becoming increasingly difficult to get you to sleep nights. You're worse than you ever were before school. I don't know, it must be all your learning—keeping you up nights."

And she started to leave. Now he must think of something else in a hurry. And he *did* think of something, suddenly. "Mom!" She paused. "Mom, why don't you like Mr. Blake?" It was just a chance, but it might detain her.

Ah, she turned, and she seemed to be smiling.

"So," she said, "what big imaginations you have."

"What's 'imaginations'?"

"Imaginations?—they're ears that don't hear and eyes that don't see. Now go to sleep. GO . . . TO . . . SLEEP!" And this time she meant it.

Outside the door, she called, "Good night—little Fox." And then she was gone. But it wasn't so bad; she didn't close the door all the way.

Sixth Chapter

THE NEXT morning Mark felt fine. He woke up all at once. The sun was high in his room, and on his face; the curtains on the windows were bright with it. Outside there were happy noises. A cart went by on the road, and he could hear the harness creaking. He listened to tell if the horse was stepping high; it was, at least, it stepped fairly high, so he had to jump up to see for sure. The cart was old and a faded red, but the horse was young, a brown horse, with a white streak in his face and his breath steaming before him. The sun in the window was warm, but Mark could tell by the horse and the crisp air that it was a cold morning. Winter, though, was not exactly here yet; he did not shiver very much.

Sometimes the morning is exciting even if you are only going to school. Mark himself could scarcely wait to wash his face and brush his teeth. He dressed as fast as he could, but this morning dressing was unpleasant; he was too good for his clothes; they didn't fit at all. As he ran downstairs, his collar undone and his hair wetted down, he seemed to be dragging his clothes behind him. Only his shirt felt good, but then fresh shirts always felt good; they're new and starchy. They chafe one's neck a little, but they are worth even that. Starched collars, however, are difficult to fasten; his fingers were never clumsier. The morning time was going, and it was the more precious because there was so little of it.

Oh, life would be pleasant, indeed, if only Judith could be less determined; if only she did not insist upon walking to school with him. If only it was someone else who lived next door, for almost every morning, Monday through Friday, Judith called to him from beneath the kitchen window. At first she called just "Mark! Oh, Mark!" But the second time she would be saying, "Come to *school*, Mark. I am waiting for you!" loud enough, too, for the whole town to hear it. But the third time was the worst of all. There would be a silent moment, a sort of ominous pause, as though she were getting air in her lungs. Then she would scream—and scream as if in genuine desperation, *"Mark! Mark!* It's late, Mark; *come to school!"*

It was really frightening, in a way, for although he knew it was coming, somehow every morning it still came as a shock. Besides, he disliked the way she called his name; it reached out and grabbed him, the way she said it. It was though he were caught where he should not have been, so that whenever she called he felt like running. And he would have run, too, except that his mother was always so polite and obliging. Every morning she had to open the kitchen window and call down to Judith that Mark would be there in just a moment.

It is easy for advanced men to understand why a young man was reluctant to walk to school with Judith. She walked slowly, of course; but that wasn't the reason exactly. And she told him that he mustn't kick up dust with his shoes, although she knew very well it was a fine sight to see, as it trailed behind, in a cloud, wherever they went. But that was not quite the reason, either. There was more objection to the matter than simply pace and dust. It was a reason he could not as yet quite understand, a sort of presentiment that in some manner Judith would bring him harm. It seemed he had already fallen under some suspicion of keeping company with girls. The injustice of that was beside the point. The situation itself was clear enough. If he failed to be wary, if he failed to avoid Judith, he would become known as a sissy, such as Rodney Fowler, a despicable fellow who shot marbles with his fingernail. That would never do. Mark realized that he had his future to consider.

As a matter of fact, he had been fair enough with Judith. He had even walked to school with her when he knew better. Occasionally he still took the risk, despite that he had been twice apprehended in her company.

"Don't you care what the boys say, Mark," she had told him; but he had to care. She failed to understand. He had tried to explain, and Judith was sympathetic, he would say that for her, but somehow, in the end, she misunderstood. Her whole solution for the problem was that he should disregard what people said. In the end, he was forced to tell her that if she must walk to school with him, the only decent way to do it was for her to walk behind him a way, as though she were not really with him, technically speaking.

Judith was obliging enough. She did walk behind. But you couldn't fool anyone like Peg Souley. He knew. In fact, they had been walking together one autumn morning when Peg came along to whistle and leer at him; then, before Mark knew what had happened, Judith stepped up and put her arm on his, to look across the street and lift her chin.

That had been a predicament. Peg told everyone, of course; and after that he kept his eye on Mark. Whenever Mark walked with Judith—when they really walked side by side—scarce as that occasion was, Peg either saw or heard of it. It was amazing. Why, they could scarcely go to the store without coming upon Peg. Judith regretted the predicament; but, really, she seemed to be unaware of its various ramifications.

Oh, Judith hated Peg enough. It was not that. She and Mark had planned what they would do one day to Peg. She said, "We'll build a little trap and he'll fall in it, and when he's in it we'll throw rocks at him and pull his hair out," she explained. As an afterthought, she added, "Then I will kick him."

Mark was not so sure. "He might run away. He might run crying to his mother."

"No," said Judith, "we will take all his clothes off him and leave him alone all night. The worms will crawl over him.

"And in the morning," she said, taking another breath, "then in the morning we will give his clothes to the poor people."

But somehow that was not to Mark the triumph it was to Judith. He feared that no matter what they did to him, Peg would still have the advantage. Mark failed to comprehend why this was so, but he knew that trapping Peg and hitting him with rocks, and perhaps squashing him, would be the wrong thing to do. It would sort of be indicative that he liked to play with girls.

"But the *worms* will crawl all over him," Judith had said. "*He'll* be sorry." Mark had refused her; and, as if her feelings were hurt, she never mentioned her plan again.

No, there seemed to be no solution for the problem. Mark frowned. He was trying to fix his collar, and his mother was calling him to come to the table. If Judith insisted upon walking to school with him, she would have to walk a way behind; that's all there was to it. He dismissed the subject and concentrated upon his breakfast.

Things were bubbling on the stove, making that plopping noise that sounded so funny. Sunlight spread through the kitchen and his mother's dress was bright; she looked like the morning. She gave him his fruit juice. It tasted good, but there was a lot of it, so much of it, indeed, that after he drank it, he had no room left for his mush. However, he had to eat his mush, and because the morning was remarkably fine, he disposed of the mush as quickly as possible. Then, with a piece of toast in his hand, he ran to the parlor, sprinted back to the kitchen to put his napkin in the napkin ring, and sprinted back to the parlor again. Somewhere in here he had left his spinning tops. The shades were drawn and the room was rather dark. Out of breath, he groped for the light.

Then he heard her, clear through the house he heard her. "*Mark!* Oh, Mark!" The neighborhood rang with her voice. It was such a sudden noise, so high and disturbing, that all at once he felt empty and confused. In the half dark he looked left and right, but he could not locate his tops. He was even looking in the same places more than once. He groped under the table three different times. Unconsciously, he was waiting for that call to come again, and even as he searched, he waited. He heard the clock, and he stumbled in the dark and fell flat against the smoking stand. In his haste, getting up, he knocked it over again, breaking in three pieces the little glass tray. He tried to fix it, so his mother wouldn't know, but he had not even time for that, for once more it came, that call:

"Come to *school*, Mark! I'm way-ting for you!"

The young man in the parlor sighed. "Judith's waiting—can't you hear her?" he heard his mother say, and then he heard her telling Judith that he would be out in just a moment. His shirt began to chafe his neck; the stocking on his left leg was slipping and, at the same time, his ear began to itch. The parlor was a dark place; the furniture in here was heavy and plush; and in the morning, he realized, the parlor was not the place to be. He hitched up his stocking, wearily squared his shoulders, and turned to go. There was no use waiting for the third call. He walked back through the kitchen, kissed his mother in a preoccupied fashion, and with his foot kicked open the back door to meet Judith.

Judith seemed unnecessarily happy. She wore a yellow ribbon, and it seemed to her that her dress in its freshness was new leaves, spreading from a branch. She looked at Mark eagerly. "It's a lovely morning," she said, tentatively; but Mark did not even look up to see whether he thought so. "I couldn't find my tops," he explained, and started for school; and she followed after, a dozen paces behind.

Seventh Chapter

BUT MARK was not the only man in Judith's life. There was a Mr. Anderson, the man whose cat had kittens. His farm was behind Judith's house. Lucky it was for him that it was there, too, for Judith kept an eye upon it and upon Mr. Anderson. He did not mind. He had lost his childless wife and he was lonely, but he stayed on his small farm after her death, sowing enough for his needs, and selling milk and eggs; and now and then he managed a payment on his place by selling a few Spring Fryers on the day before a holiday.

There was something wrong with Mr. Anderson. He was not as others were, and that got him into trouble. For one thing, he was occasionally seen down by the Savings Bank throwing dry crumbs to the pigeons that clumsily flew back and forth between the Bank and the nearby belfry of an old church. People going into the Bank with their money and their little deposit books saw Mr. Anderson, but he didn't seem to see them. They had to speak to him first. Oh, he was polite enough and he took off his hat to the ladies, but he smiled seldom; he only bowed and nodded. And, besides, he had a beard; and the beard didn't seem to be very clean.

Mr. Anderson was old but he looked strong, even though he wore an overcoat most of the time. He kept his crumbs in a crumpled paper bag in his overcoat pocket, and when he got to the Bank, he would stand there awhile, by the side facing the street, with his hands in his pockets, just waiting. The pigeons knew him and fluttered down from the church to his feet and began walking around in important little circles. Then Mr. Anderson began feeding them crumbs. They seemed preoccupied, he and the pigeons, but if any person came by and stopped to watch, the birds arose and soared away; they all left together, as if all had realized the danger at once, and Mr. Anderson raised his eyes quickly as they left, as though he would be with them. But he would have to turn and bow and put his hands in his overcoat pockets again, to wait for the intruder to go away, so the birds would return again.

When the crumbs were finally gone, Mr. Anderson folded his paper bag and placed it back in his pocket. He slapped his hands together, the pigeons flew away, and if on this trip to town he had any money, he would go into the Bank and make a payment on his farm.

On his farm Mr. Anderson kept one cow, two dozen hens, and a rooster or two, but few as his chickens were, he failed to give them the personal care that Judith believed they were entitled to. She was forced to keep a hospital for the chickens. Her mother had a piano and Mr. Blake saved the box that it came in. This was Judith's hospital. She had intended it for a doll's house, and she still talked about it becoming one, but at the moment the problem of caring for the chickens was more pressing.

Judith's hospital was equipped with little but iodine and Vaseline, and many strips of cloth from her father's old shirts; but the hospital had a picture in it that made the piano box look like a hospital. A poster, it was, showing troops marching, in the background, and in the foreground, the face of a valiant nurse. The nurse was Judith's idol, for she was not only beautiful and as clean as could be, but she had a starchy cap atop her head. There was an expression of tremendous concern on her face and she held out her arms in supplication. The printed caption on the lower part of the poster enquired: HAVE YOU ANSWERED THE RED CROSS XMAS ROLL CALL? The poster, the hospital, and the medicines were on Mr. Anderson's side of the fence, near the stile.

In the evening after school Judith crossed the stile to Mr. Anderson's farmyard to inspect the injuries of the day. The chickens were not clever. They came running as though they were going to get something to eat. If Judith saw one of them with a scratched leg or an angry comb, she had to catch it, a thin little girl in wide skirts and a red sweater, chasing an agitated chicken. And if you looked at her closely, you would have seen on her face the same expression of tremendous concern that the nurse in the poster had. Often enough, as much as Judith dreaded it, she would have to put iodine on the scratch; the chicken struggled and fussed, and in the end became very exasperated. If the chicken had to be bandaged, it would have to remain in the hospital for awhile until Mr. Anderson was shown the chicken and warned not to let it scratch off the bandage.

In all, the chickens kept Judith fairly busy, and Mr. Anderson would sometimes return from town to find half a dozen of them in the hospital, fuming and chattering, while the other hens gathered around the netting to look through, curious and startled, at the antics of the wounded.

Mr. Anderson accepted the situation courteously and wisely; he even thanked Judith for her trouble. He also told her she could come over and have a ride on his cow, and this she sometimes did.

Judith's parents did not want her, at first, to go over to Mr. Anderson's. There was something strange about him; he kept to himself. But Mark and Mr. Anderson got along fine and were old friends. Mark's father had said that Mr. Anderson was all right. "You have to get to know him," he said.

Finally, Mr. Blake talked to Mr. Anderson one evening; they discussed mortgages and Mr. Anderson's mortgage, and after that Judith could attend Mr. Anderson's chickens.

Judith's father did not know that she rode the cow; it was just one of those things that she and her mother did not mention; so riding the cow was always something of an adventure. The cow, though, was simply an ordinary cow, gentle, with eyes large and placid, as cows' eyes go, and a tail that seemed to swing back and forth most of the time. Judith could persuade the cow to give her a ride at almost any time she chose. Naturally, she couldn't direct the route, but she could lead her to the stile and climb on her back, and just sit there, occasionally urging the cow with a gentle kick to move forward a little. As a rule, though, the cow stood by the stile, tossing her head once in awhile to see if Judith was still astride her.

That cow was one of the inducements that Judith offered Mark to come and play with her after school. Now a ride on a cow was a tempting offer, and the first time that Judith gave him the invitation, the boy came gladly.

Mark had never ridden anything in his life, not even a horse, and to ride a horse was his first ambition. Of course, he had straddled an old collie dog that belonged to a neighbor; but this was not satisfactory. It was not really riding; the dog immediately sat down. But to ride a cow was another matter. He had been hearing a good deal lately of cows and cowboys. He realized well enough that cowboys didn't ride cows; but here was a cow, there was no horse; he might as well ride the cow.

It was a pale and watery afternoon in that late autumn, and the sky was about to give up its clouds. The meadow was damp with the rain that fell a few hours before, but the grass was still green, even in this season. The split logs of the stile were wet, and one had to be careful of his step.

Mark had to wear his rubbers, over his shoes, which was an indignity. When he saw Mr. Anderson coming across the meadow from his house, he hoped that he would not notice his rubbers. But Mr. Anderson himself was wearing some, holding up the legs of his trousers, as though he was wading, and as he walked toward him, Mark could see the thick white woolen socks above his heavy shoes. Mr. Anderson seemed pleased.

"Well, Mark," he said, "it's been a long time since you've visited me. Where've you been?"

"I been going to school," Mark replied.

"Oh, yes," said Mr. Anderson. "And how do you like it?" Mark told him it was the best place in the world, for that was one way of describing it.

"Have you heard from your Daddy?"

"He's going to send me a Christmas present—clear from France." France was a place beyond his imagination, as far away as they say the stars are, but his father was there, and that was the difference.

How exciting that *his* father should be in France! "I don't know what it will be," Mark told his friend, "but it'll be from the war! I'll bet it will be from the war!" he repeated, awed with the thought.

"And I'll bet my Daddy's the best shot there," he added. "And that he's getting them—Bang, bang, bang!" he cried, to show how it was done.

"You shouldn't say that," Mr. Anderson told him. "Your daddy is there for a different purpose. He's a doctor, Mark; you should be thankful he's there to help people."

Mr. Anderson was always saying things like that. Mark couldn't understand. Other people said to him all the time that they bet his father was killing a lot of Huns, but Mr. Anderson never seemed to be glad when he said things like that. And sometimes he walked around with his head down, as if he did not want anyone to talk to him. Mark looked at him uneasily.

But Mr. Anderson was rocking back on his heels and smiling at him and at Judith. "So you've come to ride the cow," he said. "Well, welcome to our meadow, Mark. Isn't that right, Judith?"

Judith said that it was right. "We've *both* come to ride the cow," she added.

"You're some buckaroos, aren't you; I said you're some buckaroos, aren't you?" You had to answer Mr. Anderson right away because sometimes he repeated things.

Both Mark and Judith nodded. "I'm going to be a cowboy," Mark added.

"I thought you were going to be a soldier. Last time I saw you, you were going to be a soldier."

"Oh, I am," Mark replied, "I'm going to be both. Were you ever a cowboy, Mr. Anderson?"

No, Mr. Anderson was never anything interesting. He wasn't even a soldier; but Mark liked to talk to him anyway.

"Come back and see me again, Mark; I said come back again and I'll show you how to milk the cow." He started to leave.

Mark didn't see any sense in learning how to milk a cow, but it was something to do, and he promised to come back sometime.

"You get me your Daddy's address," Mr. Anderson called, as he waded away through the meadow, "and I'll write him a letter."

Now at last Mark could ride the cow. Judith was leading it to the stile. It was larger than he thought it would be. Indeed, the nearer the cow came, swinging its head and slushing forward, the less he liked the looks of it. The closer it came, in fact, the less he wished to ride it. Finally, when the cow got to the stile, he definitely decided against a ride. Nor was he so sure that Judith should ride, either.

But Judith was insisting that since Mark was her guest that he should have the first ride. He could not very well tell her that he did not want to ride.

One couldn't tell a girl that. You could tell her, though, that the cow looked indisposed today and that one should not burden it further. But Judith said that the cow was perfectly fine.

"Aren't you, Bossy?" she said, for that was the cow's name, really. And she gave her a comforting pat and looked up at Mark. "Isn't she lovely?"

"No," said Mark, "look at her mouth." And it was, indeed, a very wet mouth; besides, it was large, and there was some oozy green around the under side.

"She's drooling," Judith explained. "Aren't you drooling, Bossy?" and she waited for Mark to climb on. Judith seemed to sense his reluctance.

"I'll go first," she said, brightly, "and show you how to do it."

"Oh, I know how all right," said Mark. "I'm just thinking of the cow."

"She's a nice cow," Judith replied, "and she likes to have little children ride her, don't you?" and she patted Bossy again. "My," Mark thought, "why does she always have to say 'little children'!"

But Judith was already on her way to the cow's back. She jumped from the stile and as she landed lightly on the cow, she revealed her black bloomers and her thin little knees; Mark remembered that that was another embarrassing habit of hers.

Once in the saddle, Judith smoothed down her skirts and said, "Go ahead, Bossy." Bossy did amble forward a few steps and then leaned down, her face to the meadow, for a bite of grass. Judith hung on well; she was practiced.

"See," she exclaimed, "how nice it is! And look how high up you get!"

Mark indeed did see how high in the air she was. He feared for her, but mostly because he knew that in a moment it would be he instead of Judith up there at the same extraordinary height. Even more, for he was taller.

Judith slid down into the meadow, exposing her bloomers again, and led Bossy back to the stile.

"Just jump on," she suggested, "like I did."

But the cow gave Mark a look. It was, no doubt, a mild and gently curious look, but Bossy had that large head and a large face, and that large and very wet mouth. Mark could not help but feel that there was the possibility that his head would fit in Bossy's mouth. After all, there was no accounting for cows.

"Just stand on the stile and put your leg over," Judith was saying. "Look, I'll put her right against the fence. It's easy," she added.

The situation, Mark felt, was becoming acutely embarrassing. Here was Judith telling him what to do, instead of him telling her; he could never survive this. He would never be the same with her again. Indeed, he was becoming a little angry with her. Why was she insisting he get on her old cow?

He felt that he needed time; he wished to think.

"Don't worry," he said, "I'm going to do it. I'm just doing something else right now."

"Doing what?" Judith asked, looking up at him from under the cow's neck.

Mark had to think fast. What could he be doing? He thought and thought. It was time now for an answer.

"Shush," he said.

Judith looked up at him, puzzled.

"Huh?" she said.

"I'm listening for something," Mark explained, beginning to listen.

"Listening for what?" asked Judith, suddenly concerned.

"Just listening, I told you."

Judith began to listen too. "I don't hear anything," she said, wrinkling up her nose.

"Shush," he said, "I thought I heard your mother calling."

It was very quiet in the meadow. There was scarcely a sound. Far away, beyond the town, there was a dull blasting. A bird flew by, calling. Bossy shifted her weight. That was all.

"But it's early yet," said Judith, after a moment. "Mama wouldn't call; we just got here." She paused; then she said it, and it wasn't like her, but she said it.

"Bossy—she won't hurt you," she told him.

Mark stiffened; he tried to get angry. "Who said she would?" he wanted to know. And he got one of those desperate, drained-out feelings, when he couldn't see very far in front of him and his lower lip began to wriggle. And he would do anything to stop his lip from wriggling; he would even discard his caution. The feeling was exactly what he needed for the moment, although when he contemplated the feeling later, he was not particularly grateful for it.

For now he was on the stile. Now, without stopping, he jumped. He sailed through the air, and then he landed. In fact, he had such momentum upon landing that he began to slip off the far side of Bossy, but his desperation was still with him and he grabbed hold of that broad, sleek back, trying to dig his fingers into some loose part that he could hang onto. It wasn't until a moment later that he realized that Bossy was likely to rebel against such grabbing. Mark slipped further; indeed, he was almost gone to the meadow far below, when at last he got hold and hitched himself upward, finally to get to a position where he could sit up, as though in a saddle. He released his breath again.

"Well," he said, slowly, with ease and almost with triumph, "well?" But he noticed with some alarm, now that he was no longer angry at Judith, that she was looking up at him curiously, as though she was about to have an idol destroyed before her eyes.

"Well," he said again, having nothing else to say, and believing something should be said.

"Tell Bossy to gidday," Judith said, shortly.

"Get day." But he did not say it very loudly, for

he did not know but that Bossy might think that he meant it; and even if he did give the cow a prod with his foot, it was a careful prod, and not enough of a nudge to excite anybody. But Bossy did not intend to move, anyway.

After a moment, Judith took her wondering eyes away from Mark and started to tug the cow by the halter.

But this, to Mark, was the worst thing of all. His triumph slipped from him and fear came in its place. "Don't," he cried, "don't *lead* her!" He was thinking that suppose someone—suppose Peg?—saw them, saw Judith, a girl, leading his mount.

Judith could understand this fear, as Mark quickly outlined its ramifications to her. Now that he had to get down, he didn't know just how to start. But his apprehension of danger from Bossy was completely displaced by fear of his being seen with Judith leading her. There was the thought, of course, that if he jumped from Bossy's back to fall at her feet, that she would kick, but even that would be no more of a calamity than the sight of Peg.

Bossy stood quite calmly, and Mark tried to get both legs on one side of her; but when he felt himself slipping off sideways, he did not really care; he just let himself slip. Bossy was not at all concerned with what was happening on her back. And when Mark finally reached the comfortable earth again, and stumbled, he felt no relief for his miraculous descent until he had looked right and left at the horizon and had satisfied himself that Peg, for once, was not in sight.

Then he felt very fine, indeed. His spirit was a rising bird. Life was not so bad, after all. "I'll tell you what," he called to Judith, "you get on and *I'll* lead the cow."

Judith did feel that her ride had been insufficient. She pulled Bossy to the stile and leapt on, happily, and Mark led the cow by the halter, stepping carefully, as one does when in a pasture, while Judith murmured again and again how nice and considerate he was; in return, he repeated to her just as often, so she would be sure to understand it, the ignominy of his former position aboard the cow. She must realize that a girl cannot lead a cow while a fellow is on it, especially when there is the danger that Peg may be lurking just beyond the horizon.

Yet, before he was convinced she understood completely, their discussion came to an end and words were left in the air, for they had become suddenly aware of a low droning noise coming their way from the northern sky.

"Listen!" said Mark, thrilled.

Judith listened for a moment and then replied. "Airplanes," she explained. "Airplanes from Archer's Field," and she urged Bossy forward as though nothing much would happen. But Mark himself was not to be urged. He stood quietly, listening as hard as he could.

"They're just airplanes," Judith told him again.

"Don't you think I know!" He shouted at her, for he knew more about them than she did. One or two flew over every day, from Archer's Field, where the soldiers were. Mark was hoping one of the planes would loop-the-loop; he had heard they did that, but no plane ever did it for him. Yet, even beyond that, he hoped something that he could not put into thought. It was a feeling, and almost a promise, that came and overtook him when he heard the planes absorbing the sky.

The noise was coming closer and Mark stared for the first sight in the north. Mr. Anderson, in his yard, stood looking with his back to the lowering sun. Bossy shifted her weight, uneasy with that fear animals have of the extraordinary or incomprehensible. The children, in expectation, were quiet, but the beat of Mark's heart was a hard whisper inside of him, like the quick opening and closing of lips. There was a pause on the earth around him, breathless and complete, as though even the air stood still; and Mark, with his hands to his lips, waited for that sound to overtake him, and the sky, and the meadow.

Then, all at once, they were there. The sky overhead was filled with airplanes, far more than the five he could count, all red and white, tan and blue; but in this place that had been very quiet, the planes seemed like thousands, and in that moment all dimensions were gone, for the airplanes were out of proportion to everything, so that the earth and the sky were incidental to them, so that nothing mattered in that moment except their power. Then, as quickly as they were overhead, they were gone.

The boy felt weak, as if he needed to sit down; and yet, somehow, he must have been exalted, for as the noise died away in the distance, he shouted and threw his cap in the air. All the world was his again, except that now it was a smaller world and he was a larger, more powerful, person. Even Bossy seemed insignificant; and the chickens, who had run squawking at the noise, looked silly. Mr. Anderson walked back into the house, Bossy reached for a mouth of grass, and identity came back to the meadow. It had all happened in a breath, for overhead now there was no sign that the planes had been there; the sky was as blue as before. Mark turned to Judith with shining eyes.

"Gee," he said, quietly, "what a noise." He was as awed and as proud as though he had made it.

But Judith's hands had been over her ears, all the time. "Poor Bossy," she said, frowning, "she might have been scared."

Judith patted the cow's neck. "Were you scared, Bossy dear?" she whispered; and, leaning down, she gave the cow a kiss.

"Ouaw!" Mark cried—"*kissing* a cow! Ouaw!"

But Judith did not even care. She asked Bossy if she could have a ride, and Bossy must have replied that indeed she could, for the cow ambled forward a few steps. Mark took her by the halter; he felt foolhardy and reckless now; the airplanes were still with him. Given a chance, he might even have ridden her.

So they continued their adventure, beginning again where they had left off. Judith was as immaculate as when she started, but Mark had a bruise and some mud on his knee. Dampness from the grass was creeping over his rubbers, but he did not care, for he was far in the sky. In the distance, the mountains, covered with snow, were a patient background for the green meadow below, as Judith in her red sweater hung on, and the boy led the cow, around and around.

Eighth Chapter

THE WEEK passed, and that Saturday it really rained. Mark awakened to the sounds of it, peacefully, for even though it was hissing at him, it hissed in a gentle tone; the window was streaked with water, and there was so little light in his room that he almost went back to sleep. Then he remembered it was Saturday. No school! A gust of wind rattled the shutters in an ominous manner, urging him to be up; he leapt from bed and looked out at the road, to left and to right, but as far as he could see, there was no one in sight, just rain, puddles and rivers of it, rain as far as he could see.

Mark, in chagrin, turned around sleepily and stumbled against the dresser; rubbing his eyes, he scowled across the room at a squad of tin soldiers, who stared back at him in round-eyed amazement. He picked up a handful of them, and, with a deep sigh, fell back to bed. He pitted the soldiers against each other, and even made two of them rub noses; but this morning his imagination failed him. They refused to fight. He decided to ignore them for the rest of his life, for they were the wrong kind of soldiers; they wore blue coats and red trousers, and had high yellow hats, instead of khaki suits and trench helmets, and he hated them.

When his mother came into the room an hour later, she found him sitting up in bed, looking at the pictures in a book. "You're a fine one," she said, "you had better just get up, Lazybones, or you won't get any breakfast."

"Do you think it's going to rain long?" he enquired. Even though she said no, it might rain all day, anyway; he realized that. Still, his mother should have influence somehow.

When breakfast was over, Mark brought some wood into the kitchen and carried the rest of the wood that was on the back porch to the front-room fireplace, where it wouldn't get wet. Then, his work for the day finished, he began to bother his mother. She was in the kitchen, and *trying* to get her work done, she said; but he kept asking her questions.

"Your father and you," she told him, "are just alike. Don't you know that you should leave a woman alone when she's in the kitchen?"

"What did you say, Mom?"

"I said you're a nuisance."

"But what did you say before that?"

"I said I wished I could hustle you out of here . . .

Why don't you go upstairs and straighten up your room?"

Instead Mark climbed on a chair and sat watching his mother work. There was nothing, absolutely nothing to do, that he wanted to do. With his chin in his hand, he turned his attention to the window, trying to peer through the blur of water. Nothing was outside anyway.

"Mr. Anderson has some kittens," he said, tentatively.

"I know," she replied.

"He said I could have one . . ." "Yes?" she said. "But I don't want one," he added. He thought that was a great joke, and he laughed very loudly; then, serious again, he said, "I'd rather have a dog."

"You used to have a dog; you don't remember that, do you?"

Mark remembered something about it. "Did it really belong to me—was it my dog?"

"No, but you used to play with it. It belonged to your Uncle Will; he took it to the city with him."

"I want a dog that's really mine," he said, positively; he was silent for a moment, shrouded in thought, wondering exactly what kind of a dog he would like to own. Vaguely, it was a blue-black dog with white spots. "I'd feed him myself and take him to school with me and call him Cub."

"Why—'Cub'?"

"Just because . . . But I'd call him—here, Cub, Cub—and he'd come to me running. He'd come whenever I called him and he'd be the best dog in the world!" Mark was suddenly very enthusiastic, and as happy as though he owned the dog; the chances are, he would still be talking of Cub, if the telephone hadn't rung.

"Who's it, Mom?" But she failed to reply; she was speaking into the phone, and when he enquired for the second time, she waved her hand at him to be quiet. She talked for a long time, while he thought of his dog and the rain; he must have partly listened to her, though, for among the many things she mentioned, he heard the statement that the weather *might* clear up. After she hung up the telephone, she told him that she had been talking to Isobel and that she had good news for him. Isobel was Richard's mother, Mrs. Nicholls. "If it quits raining," she told him, "you can scoot over to Richard's and play in his basement."

And as soon as she said that, she must have realized her mistake, for now it seemed that the rain would last forever, while Mark kept asking if the sky looked as if it would clear up soon. She thought that it would.

"Well, how soon?" he wanted to know.

"Pretty soon."

"How long is 'pretty soon'?"

"Oh, after lunch." But that, Mark reminded her, was ages yet. He stood by the back porch, upon one foot and then another, smelling the damp, sweet dust in the air from the apple trees.

But his mother was right. It rained all morning; the trees dripped, and the eaves on the house made throaty noises overhead, until in time the fall ended and Mark could hear only the steady drip, drip of the rain spout emptying onto the cement walk. But the ground was still too wet, his mother said, for him to leave the house. It was not until afternoon, when the sun came wanly through, that she let him go. He had to wear his rubbers and a muffler around his neck. And he had to be cautioned, again and again, to keep out of puddles.

Richard had the best basement in the world. It was large and dry; and no fruit jars were in it. There was nothing so fine as a basement without fruit jars, because when there were jars of preserved fruit you had to be careful; you had to be so careful that you could scarcely play, for if you ever forgot, you would knock one over surely, and there it would be, a mess on the floor.

Richard, though, not only had a large basement with a cement floor, but he had some tools and nails, instead of fruit jars; and, best of all, he had some boxing gloves! This was almost too much. But even more than that, he had an American army helmet made of brown butcher paper. This was the finest headgear that Mark ever saw; he coveted it so much that he would have given anything that he had to possess it. But Richard spurned all offers; he realized his helmet was priceless. As he said, it had taken his older brother all afternoon to make it. The most

Richard would do was to let Mark wear it for part of a day; this he did for the trade of three clear marbles or in return for some special service.

Mark himself had a khaki hat, such as was worn by the soldiers before they left for France, but nearly everyone had a campaign hat like that; what he wanted was a helmet—a trench helmet!—the same kind that he saw on the posters at the post-office, round and hard, with the look of a turtle's back; that was the kind he wanted. The fact that Richard had one was almost too much to bear.

For Richard was the luckiest fellow in the world. Not only did he have this basement, and this helmet (although it *was* made of butcher paper) but he had a father and two older brothers to teach him to play ball and to box with him on rainy afternoons, when everyone else had to stay home and do no more than look at books.

Richard never had to do anything alone, either. He did not even sleep alone, for his brothers and he had the same bedroom, a large, long place, with soldier-like individual beds under the windows. The Barracks, they called it; and Mark had tried to call his room the Barracks, too, but he was alone in there, so the name made him unhappy. His own bed, Mark had to admit, was big and awkward. He could pretend it was an ocean liner, but it was easier to pretend, as he lay in his own bed, that the little beds in Richard's house were motorboats. Once he cried when he pretended that Richard and his brothers were having fun after the lights went out, using their beds as motorboats, in a special voyage into the night.

Yes, and Richard had still another advantage. Somehow he did not get hurt as easily as Mark. He was smaller and rounder, and his back wasn't bony with shoulder blades; even his hair stayed combed, and in the summer his skin turned brown instead of pink. Yes, it was true, Richard was even stronger than he was, although Mark would have passed away with his face in the mud rather than say so.

It had been stated, and generally believed, that Richard could use his brother's boxing gloves whenever he pleased, although Mark imagined this was not strictly true. Still, he did have them plenty often. Indeed, it seemed that Richard had just about everything, even to a light in the basement for winter days when darkness fell so fast that you had to hurry home from school to get any playing done at all before night came.

This Saturday afternoon it was very pleasant in the basement. Outside the air was still heavy, yet it was clean and colder. The whole dome of the sky was milky, but the light was bright in the basement, and the air that came in was cold enough that it kept you jumping.

Like an attic, a basement is a secret place, slightly removed from the world, but still within sight of it; and the time that you spend there is your own and of no relation to your everyday life on the surface, for it is a secret retreat, and that is why you feel guilty when you return to the world . . . Mark had this feeling while he was in Richard's basement, so he was having a very good time, indeed, even though he was only helping Richard paint a sign for the clubhouse that they intended to build some day. They wanted to have a place of their own, for themselves and fellows they knew, a hidden place where they would be the rulers.

Their plans were many, and exciting in their complications; but even of plans they wearied after a while, both deciding at the same time that they wanted to do something besides plan for the future; so they boxed. It was perfect, the boxing; they both struck enough decisive blows that each one was able to claim that he had won. Their heads had rung and both Mark and Richard had been angry for a moment or two, but, fortunately, they had not been angry at the same time. No blood came from their noses and Richard this time had not hit Mark in that place in his stomach, for when that place was hit Mark just could not be as interested in boxing as before; at such times, in fact, he found himself thinking of reasons why they should stop. But this afternoon they seemed to stop by common consent, which was the best way; and they sat down on boxes, panting, with their hearts thumping, and tried with their teeth to undo the hard-knotted strings which held their gloves to their wrists.

Mark noted with satisfaction that the sky was almost entirely clear. That meant Richard could have dinner at his house. Afterward, in the evening, Richard's parents would come over to visit his mother. They usually did that on Saturday evenings or Sundays. Before Mark's father went to war, the families took turns coming to each other's house, but now Richard's parents usually came to his place, because their house was down by the river and they said they didn't feel right about Mark and his mother walking home all that way alone. Richard's father could walk with them, but the night air was bad for him, everyone agreed.

While Richard was walking with Mark toward his house, they decided that on next Saturday they would go pick holly berries down by the Indian River; that is, if they could get their mothers to agree.

"I know where it grows best," Richard said. "Come on, I'll show you," and they turned down a side road to walk past the ore mill, to where Richard could point out the holly bushes.

The river was a half mile away, but at the point where the boys stood it must have once been closer, for they stood on a sort of cliff, above the rocks and sandy ground below, with here and there stretches of fertile earth, that led to the water. The ore mill was built in the sandy earth that met the firm wall of the cliff.

It was difficult to see where the holly bushes were,

for the sky was beginning to darken and the sun was low enough in the west that there was a long shade from the mill to the riverside, and down in there were piles of crumbling rocks that had once been whitened with water, but now were bleached with age, so that they looked like giants hunched in the dusk. But Mark didn't say so; he was saying that Richard was crazy.

"That mill does too make cannon balls," he insisted. He knew what he was talking about; he had seen cannon balls.

"That's an iron mill," Richard replied, angrily. "It gets iron. It don't make cannon balls." But Richard had no way of proving his statements; that he seemed to realize, for he withdrew to a lofty station and from there gave Mark glances of distant superiority. He muttered that Mark certainly had crazy notions, all right.

Mark himself was not at all sure that his idea was true, but he knew better than to admit it, for in the face of Richard's superior certainty it would have been the same as an admission of defeat. Instead, he told Richard to come down and see the cannon balls for himself, and he led him down the side of the cliff to the mill, where they could see the machinery. No one was at work now, but there in plain sight were the cannon balls, dozens of them, lying one against the other on a long tread belt, each ball as large as an apple.

Richard was not impressed. "*Those*," he said,

"are *ball-bearings*, just ball-bearings. Don't you know what a ball-bearing is?"

"*Those*," said Mark, "are cannon balls."

"They're ball-bearings! Anybody knows that . . . Cannon balls look like this"—and with a stick Richard drew in the damp sand either the outline of a gunshell or a kind of modernistic pear.

Mark again was able to correct him. Down here it was getting darker, so that it was difficult for him to tell exactly what Richard had drawn, but he knew it was not a cannon ball, for he had seen many of them in books; especially did he remember the pictures of cannon balls that were bumping into the side of Old Ironsides. "Cannon balls," he explained, with severity, "are round like baseballs, only bigger and harder . . . *Anybody* knows that!" And he, too, shook his head to indicate how crazy Richard was.

But that was the end of the argument, because suddenly, together, they noticed that night had fallen. Mark looked at Richard, and Richard looked at Mark; it was kind of scary down here. They started scrambling up the bank, each hurrying as much as he could without attracting the scorn of the other. Richard went first, so that Mark was able to feel in the dark behind him various hands reaching out to pull him back to the pit . . . And when he reached the bank, out of breath, he saw in terror that a man was standing directly in his path.

Mark had not seen the man before. He seemed to have suddenly appeared there; yet, from his way of standing, he looked as though he had been waiting for them.

"Hello, boys," he said. He was standing right in the path; and when he spoke, Richard stepped back and bumped into Mark. He was so obviously frightened that Mark laughed; besides, the bump had broken the spell of the dark place they just left. Up here on the cliff, it was still daylight, and Mark felt quite a relief when he looked at the man. He was a young man, but nevertheless he was grown-up, which gave Mark confidence. He was thin, but still he looked lumpy in his brown trousers and sweater, for they were rumpled. Mark liked his hair, for it was different than any man's hair he had seen before; it was very light and moved back from his forehead in small, damp waves. He was smiling, and still standing in the path.

But Mark could not think of anything to say to him. The man wanted to be friends, but he was a man Mark had never seen before, and there didn't seem to be anything to tell him, unless he told him about the cannon balls.

"They tell me," said the man, after a moment, "that bulrushes are down by the river—bulrushes and pussy willows . . . Do you know where they are? I would like to pick some for a boy friend of mine," he added.

He was very polite. Mark was feeling sorry that he had failed to say hello to the man. He immediately pointed out where the bulrushes were. "You go right down here," he explained, "and you keep right on going past those rocks to the other rocks, past the reeds to the stale water; right there, that's where they are . . . Aren't they?" he said, turning to Richard.

"But I'm a stranger here," the man told him. "I wouldn't be able to find them alone . . . Now if one of you will take me to where they grow, I will do something for you—I will give you ten cents."

Mark looked at Richard, but Richard shook his head. "I won't go," he said, loudly; and he left the path to start to walk around the man.

"Oh, you're not afraid of me, are you?" the man said. But Richard did not reply. "Why, I wouldn't hurt you," the man told him. "You don't think I'd hurt you, do you?"

Richard shook his head. Mark thought that Richard had hurt the man's feelings. He was angry that Richard acted like that. "Come on," he said to Richard, "let's show him where they are. We still got time."

"Now there's a nice boy," said the man. "And if your friend don't want to go, he don't have to. You can show me and have the dime all for yourself!"

"No, thank you, Sir, I don't want any money," Mark replied, in the tone he used for talking to grown-up strangers. But he did wish he had ten cents all his own.

He asked Richard again. "Don't you go," Richard told him. "If you do, I'll go home."

But the man had already taken Mark's hand and was leading him down the path. "Come on," Mark called back. "Please!" But it didn't do any good; Richard wasn't coming with him. "Wait for me, then!" he yelled. "We'll be right back!"

The man had a large hand, and Mark's own hand felt very small in it. He tried to get his hand loose, but the man held it tighter, and smiled down at Mark.

"It's dark down there," Mark said, and stopped.

"Oh, don't pay any attention to a little thing like that," he was told. "I'll get my shoes muddy," Mark said; and when the man didn't reply, he added, "This is all the further I'm going. I'm going home now."

"Well, let's sit down here a minute," the man said, pointing to a large rock. "It isn't dark here."

"I'm going home now," Mark repeated. But the man sat down. "Wait just a minute." He was talking politely. He put his arm around the boy's waist and drew him down to the rock. Mark didn't like that, but the man was smiling.

"That's a nice muffler you have on," he told Mark, and fingered it. "I'll bet it keeps you good and warm."

"It's my mother's," Mark explained. "She made it and gave it to me."

"You're a fine boy, then," the man said, and smiled again. He had a funny way of smiling, for when he smiled he didn't open his lips, he only drew them closer. "I think I'll tell you a story," he said. "I tell fine stories."

Mark did not want to hear a story; he had to be home. It was almost time for supper, but he could not be so rude as to tell the man he did not want to hear his stories. "Well," said the man, "once upon a time . . ." and as the story started, Mark suddenly knew that the man's arm was stealthily tightening around his waist.

"*Don't* do that!" Mark shouted. He was surprised that he had said it so loudly, and he really didn't know why he said it . . . But now he knew he was going home. "You let me go," he said, and he meant it so much that the man did let him go.

Mark started walking away; he wanted to run hard, but he did not want the man to think that he was afraid.

"I'll give you lots of money," the man called to him. "Fifty cents!" he said, in a hoarse whisper.

Mark looked back, thinking the man might be right behind him, but he was still sitting on the rock. "I'm going home," he said.

"Yes," the man nodded, "go home . . . Go home like a good boy."

Mark never forgot it, he said it so softly, but the words seemed to release a tension in the boy, for he started running as fast as he could, as though his legs were his will to carry him home; up the bank and beyond the cliff, he was still running, oddly detached from his body, so that he was watching his legs, weightless and free, flying beneath him. And almost before he knew it, his house was in sight; he slowed down then, out of breath, and glanced back to see if the man was in sight, but it was too dark for him to see that far. He was aware now of what had happened, and the heaviness of gravity returned to him; he was very tired, and he tried with his hands to his mouth to stop his sobs, but they came anyway, so hard they seemed to shake him.

As Mark started trotting, looking for Richard and trying not to cry, he saw the first light when it appeared in his house. He trotted faster. It was the kitchen light, and it came on to encourage him. He ran through the backyard and stopped by the door a moment to get his breath; he wanted to run right in the house to his mother, but somehow he felt that he had done something very strange and very wrong. For the first time in his life he was afraid to tell his mother. He could not understand why, nor did he try to understand; it was simply that there was something wrong, and he felt ashamed.

But all that his mother said was that he was late. She wasn't angry; she said that just as a greeting. Then she noticed that Richard was not with him.

"But isn't he coming at all?" she asked. Mark did not know what to say. He was going to tell her about the bulrushes and the man, but he didn't know how to begin. He wanted to, but he couldn't; he felt ashamed.

"What's the matter with you?" she asked, but before he could reply, she said, "So you two have been arguing. Is that it?"

"No," Mark said, and he felt miserable.

"You look awfully tired, Baby," she said. "You shouldn't play so hard; you're not strong enough." And she put her arm around him and took off his cap, to brush his hair back from his forehead. "And crying, too," she said. He hung onto her tightly, but everything was so warm and safe here in the kitchen that he just couldn't say a thing.

Ninth Chapter

MARK WAS not often indifferent to those things in his life that reached beyond his comprehension. It was the furthest one, hanging from the tip of the most slender limb of the tree, that was his apple. He had to grope for it, to hold it as his own, until it felt familiar in his hand. For even the stars were not too far; he need but wish hard enough. Lucky for him, before he ever tried to cause a star to fall, he saw another apple.

So it was that whenever something happened which Mark could not understand, he was drawn to it until his curiosity was satisfied; indeed, perhaps until he burned his hand. Yet there were times when he felt a force within him greater even than curiosity, and that force, too, which bid him to be careful, was strong when things happened that he failed to understand. It was as if he had never seen the flame before, and was fascinated by it, but realized in the back of his mind that it would burn.

When between these forces, Mark was cautious; he moved on tip-toe, as though a sense had fore-warned him that something occurred which he must shun. He kept clear of this thing, moving thought-fully and carefully, aware of the apple's fascination, but bewaring of the mysteries of the serpent. Once in his life Mark had a chance to look at a dead man, but his uneasiness was a dread greater than his curiosity. It was a relative who had died, and that relative had been kind to the boy; Mark had liked him very much, but as soon as the man was dead, Mark shunned all thought of him. Nothing could have forced him to look.

Even in such a manner as a child will shun the dead, both Mark and Richard avoided mentioning the man who wanted bulrushes. They were both too young to comprehend his intention, yet Mark, at least, avoided the subject as much as if he had known. Like the dead, it was unmentionable.

Their parents, seeing them playing together that evening, evidently decided the children had an argument and now were slowly and thoughtfully becoming friends again, for they left them alone. Furthermore, not once that week at school did either Mark or Richard refer to the iron mill, the basement, or their painted sign for the clubhouse they planned, for an imaginary circle was drawn around that Saturday, and neither boy stepped over it. They even played again at Richard's house the next week-end, but if an adult had been there, he would never have known that they possessed a secret.

In fact, they were almost forced together, for their mothers, as matrons of the community, were requested to attend a meeting. The elders of Colburn had decided to meet in the town hall that afternoon and settle a problem of utmost importance. The nation had been drinking too much. Fathers were spending their salaries in saloons and coming home for dinner at a late hour. All over the nation fathers were acting in this manner, and all over the nation meetings were held to think of something to do about it. For a moment the war was forgotten. Drink was now definitely considered an evil, this fall of 1918; there was talk that one day there would be a prohibition against it.

Mark had heard much of this problem, but it failed to disturb him. It concerned him only in that all talk by adults took up his mother's time when she could have been doing something worthwhile with him, for people interrupted their walk to speak to her, and as often as not the subject was drink and the contemplated prohibition against it. That was all that he had against drink and he heard of it only when he was tugging at his mother's hand, urging her to continue with him wherever they happened to be going. He never knew that it was drinking when his mother poured his father's wine into those little glasses.

Therefore, because of drinking fathers and an

earnest young organization called the Women's Christian Temperance Union, Mark and Richard were left at Richard's house with a house-keeper named Christina, a large woman with a rolling bosom and a determination to stand for no nonsense. Christina would give them their lunch, milk, some squares of cheese and cookies, and a lumpy vegetable that lay insolently in pale green water. Mark pretended it was a frog.

"Now be good boys," Richard's mother had said, in warning. "Eat your lunch when you are hungry, but don't drop crumbs on the floor—and *don't* play in the street."

Then, putting her handkerchief in her purse, she straightened her stiff afternoon-dress, and left the house with Mark's mother. Mark watched them walk up the street, and then they were gone.

He was left with nothing to do. Richard had to take his bath and Christina went in with him to make sure that he used the soap. Mark stood at the window and looked out at the street, which lay sleeping in the sun; he was trying to solve a problem of his own.

When you are very young it is difficult to think about things for any length of time. Sometimes you try to think something through, but another thought comes breaking in, and then before you know it, you are out of the house and running.

But Mark did not run very far, only to the gate, where he leaned, listening, for he thought he heard

Richard yelling in terror. Yes, Richard was complaining; Mark was happy to hear him. But he still had his problem. What if he should never see his mother again? Suppose something happened. He had kissed her before she left; that was not his worry, for kissing was a charm that broke the spell of good-bye. Yet, he felt that perhaps he had lied to her; and perhaps now she was gone for good, for if a kiss took away the bad of a good-bye, perhaps a lie would put it back again. Mark was trying to think hard if he had lied to her.

There was this story of the man in the bulrushes, and that was a weight upon him; but the worst of all, the lie may have been, was that she asked him that evening where Richard was, and he had replied that he did not know. This was a lie, and yet it was not a lie, for he hadn't really known; on the other hand, he had known more than he said.

It was rather comforting, though, to feel that he had not lied for certain; there was a chance that he may have but fibbed. If he fibbed, he would be forgiven. That presence in the air above him, in his body, and all about the earth; that heavenly and mysterious presence known as God, who for some obscure reason looked vaguely like Mr. Anderson— that presence everybody knew, but no one knew well —that God who had a beard; he would realize surely that a fib could come loose from an excited tongue. So if he had fibbed, he would be forgiven; there was no doubt about that. A fib did not come from him; it was the fault of his body, and Mark was not his body. His body belonged to him, true, but he was, personally, a soul and a heart; and his body was only partly his responsibility. It was all very confusing, and he would have much preferred to do something else than think; but this much he knew—a lie was the deliberate work of his soul, and it was awful. Mark did not wish to believe that his soul had been at fault.

Men good and true did not lie. His father, for one, had never told a lie in his life, and neither did George Washington, a fine man with a big head and a blue coat. No, George Washington was a liar once, but that was when he was younger than Mark. Besides, he had atoned for his lie by cutting down a cherry tree, or by some such industry. That is why good men never lied anymore, because it was a sin to cut down a cherry tree, but if you lied you had to cut down the tree; that was the rule.

Now for certain, Mark realized that he was not a liar. Yet his certainty needed to be communicated to someone else. Other people should know of his goodness. But there was no one to tell; that was the trouble. If his mother were here right now, he would assure her; then he would no longer have cause to feel that he had lied—but with his mother gone, he was not so sure . . .

Mark realized there was no use trying to tell Christina; she talked so funny he could not understand what she said. Judith would have been of some help, but she was not here. And Richard wouldn't do at all; he jumped around too much. Besides, he was taking his bath; and he was such a baby that he was afraid of soap. Therefore, all that Mark could do was lean against the gate and sigh. Life was becoming complicated.

Even when Richard joined him, Mark failed to feel any happier. They speculated upon what they should do, now that they had an entire afternoon to do it in. They realized it should be something special. Neither boy would suggest boxing, for that would have meant the basement, and somehow they couldn't go there. Richard slumped down on the porch steps; he looked pale from so much scrubbing, and his hair was still damp. Mark disliked the smell of it, without realizing why; when he smelled it, though, he remembered a wet day when he was walking along with this large man who was his uncle. His uncle was carrying the spotted puppydog and for some reason Mark was crying.

After a moment Mark turned to Richard and said, "You got a funny smell. Your hair smells."

But Richard was not in the least offended. "I wish I had a knife," he said, wistfully, not so much to Mark as to the air.

"I wish I had one, too," Mark replied.

"We could make things," Richard added, "whistles and things."

Mark considered the statement for a moment. "It would have to be a *sharp* knife," he said, for once he took a paring knife from the pantry; it wouldn't even cut wood.

"I'd want a white-handled pocket knife," Richard explained, still speaking to the air.

"You mean—pearl-handled," Mark corrected him, although he hadn't the slightest idea of what it was; he had heard the word somewhere.

"I mean white-handled," Richard replied, for he knew what he wanted.

Silence came between them on the porch, and for almost a minute they just sat and said nothing. Then Mark got up and jumped over a step. "Would you like to play marbles?" he asked, and jumped another step.

Richard sat where he was; he did not intend to play marbles. It was fun to play marbles at school, where the bell was likely to ring any moment, ending all joy. At home, where time had leaden feet, Richard chose to play something more elaborate.

But they could think of nothing to do, until Christina appeared and they went in to lunch. Mark enjoyed eating at Richard's house, if he ate in the kitchen. It was a different kind of kitchen than he had at his house. It was browner. Somehow, when you sat in it, you felt different than you did anywhere else. The table was a heavy wood, darkened, and it had a low rumbling in its thickness. You felt that if you laid your ear against it there would be noises low and faraway, as if great brown animals were running across a dark plain.

The kitchen also had a dipper. It was a large nickel one and everyone in the family drank from it. Cold water chilled the dipper, a quick and light pain across Mark's lip, so that he could not drink much water from it, but what he could drink was better than ice-water.

Richard's father had more to do with this kitchen than Mark's father did in his mother's place. For one thing, over in the far corner were his boots. And his cup and saucer were on the polished sideboard, for they were special dishes that no one else could use. Mark knew what he did with them. Every morning he filled the cup, and it was a large cup, with steaming coffee, and then he broke bread into the coffee. But he drank the coffee as though it were soup, with a spoon. Richard said that his father always did that and that he did it the first thing in the morning. It was a bad thing to do because it made him nervous; but until he did it, there was no use speaking to him. Afterwards, he was jolly enough, packing in wood or doing something necessary to his automobile. Later, he ate breakfast with the rest of the family; and if one of his sons was too sleepy to eat, he would tickle him.

Oh, it was very pleasant to have lunch in Richard's kitchen and to think about these strange things. And it was good to eat from strange plates. Even the milk tasted different and the glass that it came in was thicker. At home Mark seldom ate cookies; there was generally a box of them on the shelf, but he seldom touched them; now, though, with the cookies rationed out, two for each boy, Mark ate his and relished them.

He was beginning to feel better. He looked around the room and at the boots. He wished that his father kept boots in the kitchen, oily and smooth like those. "But my father's got better ones," he said, aloud.

"Better what?" Richard asked, wiping his mouth.

"My father's got better boots than those."

"Your father has not," Richard replied, instantly alert for an insult. He glared at Mark over his second cookie.

"Oh yes," Mark was forced to tell him. "My father's are better." That definitely settled the matter so far as Mark was concerned. But for good measure, he added, "My father said so." He did not realize he was lying.

"Say!" Richard exclaimed, as though struck by a tremendous thought, "those boots are the best boots in the whole world." And to clench his point, he added, "You bet!"

Mark was not awed; he shook his head.

"Why aren't they?" Richard demanded to know.

But Mark could not tell him. He simply shook his head once again. Almost unconsciously he seemed to know the tactics for this kind of an argument.

"Just tell me why they aren't?" Richard repeated; but Mark did not reply.

"They are too better!" Richard shouted. But still Mark declined to comment.

Almost desperate, his uneaten cookie still in his hand, Richard called Christina, who came from the pantry. But she only shrugged her shoulders and left the kitchen. Mark immediately took it as a denial.

"Ho," he said, "I told you so!"

Richard became very desperate. He dropped his cookie and ran over to the boots. He wiped his face with his hand, breathing hard. "Your father couldn't even wear these!" he screamed. "They're too heavy for your father!" and he lifted one up to indicate how heavy it was.

"Ho, Ho," Mark replied, in an insulting laugh.

Richard brandished the boot. "I'll *kill* you with it!" he said, and then changed his mind, dropping the boot with a bang. "Your father's a sissy!" he said.

That was an insult. His father a sissy! His dear father—the best doctor in the world, a sissy!

"My father," Mark told him, drawing himself up to an extraordinary height, "*is not* a sissy . . . He's a soldier, and that's more than your father is . . . And you had better just not say any more about my father." Mark told himself that he was very angry; why, he was so angry he could scarcely see across the room to Richard.

"Well," said Richard, and he backed up a little,

"Mr. Blake's kind of your father—and he's a sissy!"

"Ho, Ho!" said Mark, "what a liar!" There now, he had really called him a liar. That was an awful thing to say. He waited for Richard to charge.

"Well," said Richard again, as if he had not even been called an awful name, "he's a sissy and he's kind of your father . . . My mother said he's kind of your father.

"And don't you call my mother a liar," he added.

It was suddenly very quiet in the kitchen. Mark inspected Richard, conscious that his eyes were narrowed in a threatening manner, for ever since the argument began, he had the feeling, stronger and stronger, that he was looking outward upon himself, controlling this outward self. He must have been enjoying within the cruelty that had caused Richard's chin to drop and his eyes to widen until they were round with alarm, because he consciously decided to give him such a look that he would tremble with terror. But even as he decided, the mood within him changed, he became one with himself, and he was back in the kitchen again, shaken, wishing he were Richard's friend once more. He heard a drop of water fall from the faucet and gurgle as it ran down the sink. Richard should know he was sorry.

But Richard failed to realize that Mark no longer cared to see him squirm; Richard was groping for a fresh insult; and finally he broke the tension by

saying, a little defensively, "You're a bad boy . . .
And I'll never play with you again—never!"

"Don't be mad," Mark said, without giving it
the proper emotion. He wanted to say he was sorry,
but the words were not there.

Richard refused to be friends again; in fact, he
said, "You go home and get out of my kitchen!"

Mark remained where he was, and Richard
looked around the floor, as if for a stick, but in the
end chose a saucer. He picked it up and made horrible gestures.

"You'd better not," Mark told him.

"You go home!" Richard warned him.

"So you don't want to be friends . . . You want to
be mad. Then I wouldn't have you for a friend . . .
And I wouldn't have your father for my father . . .
and I wouldn't have you for anything, for *anything*
. . . And I wouldn't have your mother—or your old
trench helmet!" Mark had found words for his
tongue, even though they were not the words he
intended.

"You're not very smart," he added. "I'm going
home," and he did pretend to go.

"Go ahead," Richard replied, "who cares?"

"I don't even want to be in your house any
more."

"I don't want you in my house any more."

"Don't worry, I don't want to be in your house."

"I suppose," Richard began, and he paused with
the thought, "I suppose you're going to tell your

mother." He glared. "You're a tattle-tale if there ever was one."

"No, I'm not!" Mark told him. ". . . But don't think you could make me tell her," he added. Richard replied with another glare.

"If you don't look out," Mark warned him, "I'll go home."

"Go ahead!" Richard shouted. He shouted it very loudly. "I hate you anyway!" His lower lip began to twitch; Mark immediately noticed the difference. "Ho!" he intended to say, "you're going to cry." But he did not say it; he considered for a moment, and decided against it.

Then, to the boys' alarm, there was the noise of coming footsteps; the kitchen door swung open. It was Christina. She found them facing each other, across the kitchen, sullen. Mark looked at Christina and immediately sat down; Richard as suddenly became preoccupied with the toe of his shoe.

"Well," said Christina, in a voice weary with knowledge; "well," she repeated, and folded her arms, "what you fight about now?"

Richard looked up at her and his eyes widened. He did not seem to comprehend what she had asked. After a pause, in which she failed to repeat her question, Richard turned to Mark. "We weren't fighting, were we?"

Now Mark was in for it. If he agreed with Richard, he would have told a lie; if he denied it, he would betray Richard and prove that he was a tattle-tale. He decided that Richard meant more to him than Christina; and with his eyes down, he shook his head, to indicate he agreed with Richard. But Christina was not watching him. She did not see his lie; in that case, there was no lie.

She was clearing the table. "Olaf's coming," she said.

Olaf was her son—a big fellow. He was in high school and he could pitch baseball; and he had hair that looked like dirty cotton, only you had better not say so.

Olaf came into the room, carrying an armful of groceries. He set them down on the drainboard and swung his hand at the boys. "Hey, kids," he said.

Richard spoke up. "Hello, Olaf," he said; but Mark said nothing.

"So you were fighting, huh?" he asked. "Well, who licked who?" He looked at Richard. "Did you take him?" he wanted to know.

Mark felt angry, without knowing quite why, at Olaf and his questions; he had not challenged Christina's right to ask such questions, but somehow Olaf was different.

"Richard!" Christina said, sharply, and Richard looked up at her, his eyes widening in surprise. "No more fighting," she told him, and left the room.

Olaf remained, though; Mark resented his presence. "Let's go out and play," he said, pointedly, to Richard.

"Yeh, before you get to fightin' again," Olaf told them.

"We weren't fighting," Mark replied. "We were talking like a fight."

"Pretty loud talk, I'd say—from such a pair of little shavers."

Richard walked over to Olaf, so that they stood on one side of the kitchen, with Mark, their enemy, on the other. "He said my father's boots weren't any good," Richard said, "and they are, aren't they?" Olaf agreed with him. "Sure, sure," he said.

If Richard would tell, then Mark would tell, too; but for a moment he could think of nothing to tell. Then he remembered, all at once. "He said that I was a sissy. He said"—and Mark took a deep breath—"he said that Mr. Blake was a sissy and that I was a sissy because Mr. Blake is like my father!"

"I didn't!" Richard said.

"You did! You said he was kind of like my father."

"Don't tell me," said Olaf.

"But that's what you said," Richard said to him. "You said they were kind of like that."

"You kids get funny ideas. Just because I told you that when his mother was a girl she used to step out with him, don't mean they're sweet on each other . . . Kids sure get funny ideas."

"Hah," said Mark, turning to Richard in triumph. "I told you so!"

Richard looked confused. "Go on out and play," Olaf told them. "I got to fix the sink."

They walked to the front yard, a great silence between them. Richard opened the gate and swung back and forth on it thoughtfully.

"It's your turn now," he said to Mark, jumping off to let his friend ride, which was not very much like Richard. Mark rode for awhile, but it was not really a pleasure. He wanted to speak to Richard, but he did not know just what to say. He also meant to tell him that he thought his father had very good boots, providing Richard did not mean that talk about Mr. Blake and the sissy part.

Richard maintained the silence. The gate creaked back and forth. Mark finally jumped down.

"Your turn," he said to Richard.

"Thanks," Richard replied, climbing on again.

The afternoon was almost over now; the sun was already dropping in the distance, and the weather became slightly colder. Mark buttoned his sweater to the neck and thoughtfully kicked the fence with his toe.

There was the sound of heavy wheels crunching gravel in the distance. Richard listened. "Must be four o'clock," he said. "Here comes the brewery wagon." He nodded at Mark.

That was good news. The brewery wagon was the finest one in town, excepting the fire wagon, of course. It was not only the biggest and the heaviest, but it was drawn by six white horses. Oh! they were wonderful horses; their names all began with the letter *B*. There were Bill, Bart, Boston, and Boss; and then there were Baby and Beatrice, the lady horses.

The driver was named Harry. He had no other name, so far as Mark knew. No one ever called him Mister anything; just Harry. Sometimes he would give the boys a ride, but they were older boys, naturally, really advanced fellows of twelve and thirteen. Mark looked forward to the day when he would be invited to sit up on the seat beside Harry. That day was distant, he knew; still, it was very pleasant to wave at Harry now, and to have him wave back, as though they were sharing together the anticipation of a pleasure to come.

Harry himself always waved back, but the older boys with him seldom did. That was to be expected, of course. Aware of their superior position, they did not care to be familiar. Still, sometimes they waved. There was always that chance.

The truck was rumbling down the hill from behind Richard's house, coming faster the nearer it came. Harry was pulling back on the brake. But he still had one hand that was almost free; and when Mark and Richard yelled, Harry waved back with his reins.

The side door of Richard's house burst open and Olaf came running out. "Hey, Harry," he shouted.

"Wait for me!" He sprinted past the boys without looking at them, ran along with the wagon for a moment, and then leapt on.

There was another boy on the seat already. Mark saw Olaf turn to him and speak in a grave tone. He waved good-bye to Olaf, but Olaf did not see him.

"Good-bye!" Mark shouted.

The truck was way down the street by then, but Harry heard him, and turned to wave again. Mark wriggled with pleasure. He felt sure that someday Harry would give him a ride, on that day he became as old as Olaf.

Tenth Chapter

A WEEK or two later, when Mark was much older, he had a revelation. That day at school the teacher told the class that they were human beings and that human beings think. She said that thought was a wonderful thing, and that everyone thought all the time; even a child thought. One boy had raised his hand and asked Miss Matthews if he, too, could think.

"Why of course," she told him. "You couldn't even raise your hand if you had not thought about it first."

The boy had looked around the room, nodding his head and smiling. Mark moved his own arm a little, and then looked at it steadily. He knew that he could think, but he never dreamed that he could think that much.

Thinking was much on Mark's mind that afternoon, when school was over. He stood alone in the parlor, awed and sad. There was nothing for him to do. He realized that there was no reason for his grief, that no one had hurt his feelings, and that if he had something to do he would feel fine. But he stood in the parlor, aware that he was thinking. Now that he was able to think, he thought of how unhappy he was.

He was really two people. He was one person, standing by the window, in the parlor; and he was another person, who watched this one by the window. That sight made Mark very unhappy. He watched himself as he stood thinking and thinking. Since that afternoon at Richard's house more than a week had passed; it was nearly two weeks ago that Richard and he met the man who wanted bulrushes, and it was easily a month ago that Mark had ridden Mr. Anderson's cow; school was no longer the adventure it once had been. One hour was beginning to look like another, and time itself moved so slowly that the days seemed to be dragging their feet. Mark sighed for something to happen.

He did not know exactly what was the matter. Perhaps no one lately was paying him much attention. His mother was way off in some part of the house; but, even so, her stories were not as exciting as they once were. He wished that he were grown up and going to high school.

Through the window, he could see Judith playing on the road in front of her house. It was getting dark in the front room and there was not much light outside, either. If Judith did not look out, she would get caught in the night. Nevertheless, she was playing and having a good time; he wished that he could think of something to do. He even wanted to run out and play with Judith, but something held him back each time that he started. He had intended to play with Richard, but Richard lived so far away his mother refused to let him go. There was not very much to do, Mark reflected, and this was Friday night, the kind of night that let him stay up longer. Again, Mark began to see himself in the third person; he saw himself clearly in his mind as he gazed sadly out of the window, and for himself his heart was filled with pity.

He thought, for some reason, of an earlier afternoon, weeks ago, when he was much younger. He had been returning from school, somewhat pensively stepping from one crack to another in the sidewalk. The game was his own and it had rules that must be followed. There were really no penalties for skipping a crack, but the threat of them was so weighty that if he imagined he had skipped a crack he had to hop back to make sure, for skipping a crack was against the rule, and that rule must never be violated.

Intent this afternoon upon his game, Mark leapt from crack to crack very grimly, taking big jumps and small, careful jumps; he was thrilled, he was leaping in such a wonderful manner. Finally, though, he came to the place where he had to leave the sidewalk for the dirt path up the hill to his house. But he did not wish to leave the fine sidewalk this day; ahead of him were many fascinating cracks that beckoned onward. He paused to consider the situation, both feet carefully balanced on a crack. It was not late and there was nothing for him to do at home; Richard was at the dentist's and Mr. Blake was still at school. If he went home, he would have no fun for at least an hour. On the other hand, if he followed the cracks in the sidewalk for three more blocks, he would be near the main street of town; he could walk home up the road. Perhaps he would meet Mr. Anderson; but he would be sure to meet the bulldog. The bulldog bit people. However, the cracks were worth the risk.

Mark continued onward for two blocks in this leaping fashion. At one time he was desperate; he feared he would be unable to jump to a crack that was farther away than he was long. He stepped backward two cracks, which was fair under the circumstances, and then ran ahead hard. He left the last crack and flew through the air; and he made it. Out of breath, he paused and noticed that some children were playing nearby on the lawn of a large house. The house, he believed, belonged to Mr. MacKelsey, who drove a big black car back and forth to the dredgers. But Mark did not know the children; why, some of them were really just kids; he saw that at a glance. They were probably too young to be allowed in school. He should not bother with them, but he stood watching them idly, listening to the shrill, happy sounds of their voices.

The voices, somehow, were irritating; and the children themselves seemed senseless, running into each other joyfully, to fall down with a bump. He wondered what on earth they were playing; but whatever it was, he imagined that he could do it much better; indeed, he decided that not only could he run faster than they could, but he could bump harder. He decided that he would join them and demonstrate his speed and strength.

Some of the girls noticed him; they gathered together on the lawn, in their white dresses, in a secretive little circle.

"Can I play?" he called to them.

There was no reply except the echo of his own voice that came back to him from the house. The lawn became very quiet, as the children all stopped to stare at him. Someone skinny in a white dress giggled.

Mark became as casual as possible. Slouching up to the iron fence, he put his hands on the bars. He heard a murmur of alarm from the circle of girls; he decided, therefore, that he would scare them. He was not so sure, though, for he thought he heard someone whisper "street boy," in a sort of hiss.

One of the boys, the boldest, stepped forward and put his hands on the fence grilles. He watched Mark, warily. "Who're you?" he asked, after a moment.

"I go to school," Mark explained, for that should establish him as superior to the others.

"What's your name?" the boy said, and glanced back at the girls, who giggled again. "Cat's got his tongue," one of them said.

Mark drew himself up as tall as possible. "My name," he said, abruptly, "is Mark and I live on the hill," and then he paused, for he remembered Peg. "My name," he said, "I mean my name is Puddin . . . Puddin'n Tame—ask me again and I'll tell you the same! Hah, hah!"

The skinny girl shrieked and threw her arms around a friend. "His name's Pudding!" she cried. "Pudding, Pudding," she repeated, and they all laughed, to stare at him some more.

But Mark had another idea. He put his face against the iron grilles to face the boy.

"Get away from my fence," the boy said, "or I'll call John." John was evidently the gardener. Mark took his hands from the fence, but enquired, "Are you playing house, little boy?" He made sure that his voice had a tone of condescension.

The boy looked at him levelly; he seemed to be thinking. Mark returned the stare. Then one of the girls shouted.

"Go away," she told him, shortly.

Mark did not feel right about that. "I just want to play," he explained. He looked almost desperately, from the boy to the girls.

Then the littlest child of all stepped forward. "Go

'way, Bad Boy," he said. He was a tiny fat thing with a red face and dirt around his mouth; he waved his grubby hand at Mark. "Bad Boy, Bad Boy!" he yelled, and looked to his elders for approval.

"*Say!*" Mark began to bristle. He doubled up his fists, not that he would have hit the little boy, but that he would hit the one by the fence, hoping it would somehow hurt them all. But they all laughed. The boy at the fence withdrew to the comfort of the girls, and Mark did not know what to do. He looked at them steadily for a moment, even as Peg looked at him when he was with Judith; but in the end he had to walk away; he had to walk with dignity. He could no longer jump from one crack to another, not when he could feel their eyes upon him; this was no time to risk appearing awkward. He expected that a rock would follow him, but none did; he was almost disappointed.

When Mark reached the end of the block, he dared to look back; but they were far away, and he was sorry to see that they were playing again. Such indifference! He stood at the curb and kicked it thoughtfully with his foot. He could hear again their loud, thin cries of happiness that became shrieks of delight when someone fell down. He listened carefully to their voices, they were sometimes commanding and sometimes alarmed; but the largest sound of all was that of happiness; yet in them he could not detect any pity.

Now as he stood by the window, looking out at

Judith, Mark felt quite badly. He should have done something to those kids down there. No doubt he should have hit that boy in the nose. Then the mother would have come out of the house running; she would have screamed at him, and he would have dared her to let the boy come out and fight him like a man. But it was too late now.

That was in the long ago, but there was still a long time until Christmas. There was nothing to do. School had not been very good this week; now that it was over for awhile, he was not sorry. In fact, he had looked forward a little to the fun he would have over the week-end, but here it was and he was having no fun. He felt like doing something that he should not do, something he had never done before, something new. Here he was, ready, but no folly came to his attention. For a moment he considered running away, but that would not do; it was almost night time. Where would he sleep?

Judith seemed to be having a good time. She had taken her kittens for a ride. One of the kittens was supposed to be his, but he didn't want it. Judith could have them both; it was all right with him, for they were for sissies.

She had bundled them into a wagon that Mr. Anderson had built for her; the air was nippy, she had wrapped them both into an old scarf, placed them in the wagon, and drawn them around and around the road. She often did that. In fairness, and rather than hurt the feelings of Mr. Anderson's dog, a rather surly airedale, she would bundle him up, too, and drag him by the collar from his yard to give him a ride. Sometimes he sat in the wagon for awhile, distant and moody, but as often as not he jumped out as soon as Judith pushed him in. Mark regarded the whole thing as absurd.

"That dog don't want a ride," he had told her, again and again. "He does too," Judith would reply. "Don't you, dear?" she would ask, wrapping her arms around the airedale.

The thought of Judith reminded Mark of something important—that this was Friday. Twice in his life his mother had taken him to the show on the evenings of this day. Some Friday nights Mr. Blake had to work at school, so that twice Judith and her mother and Mark with his mother had gone together to the Opera House. It was all right if they came home a little late because there was no school the next day.

The arrangement would be an excellent one except that Judith had to be with him. It was not so much that he minded, but her presence had been remarked among his friends, even though the second time he had sat down front, away from her. He recalled with wry distaste the morning that followed that evening, for Judith had tried to kiss him. "Love me!" she cried, and threw herself upon him.

Still, he did enjoy the show. He would like to go again.

Mark dropped the window drapes and ran

through the house to his mother upstairs. He felt very well now, and very anxious. He found her counting the linen from the laundry, and he ran to her and put his arms around her waist.

"Mom!" he shouted, "let's go to the show tonight!" He knew she liked to go. Besides, she looked happy when she saw him. She asked if he knew what photoplay was at the theater, but before he could bring her the newspaper to find out, she stopped him.

"I don't think we ought to go out at night alone," she said, "although I would like a breath of air."

"Take Judith and her mother," he told her, promptly.

She looked at him for a moment, as though considering, but then she shook her head.

"Oh, please, Mom."

"Besides," she said, "I don't think those motion pictures are good for growing boys."

"Oh, Mother!" He could see that she was willing to listen, but he could not tell if she would agree. "It will be a very good night," he said. "And the stars will be remarkably bright."

"They will, will they? The stars will be remarkably bright. Fancy that . . . but I think the night will be cloudy and the moon will be afraid to ride so high."

Some way that the light came into the room, he could see his mother as he had never seen her before. For the first time in his life he consciously looked at her. He realized in surprise that she was a woman, like Miss Matthews, like Mrs. Blake; only she was his mother, too. He wanted to tell her of herself, but there was no way to say it. It was just some way that the light came in, and some way that she looked at him, holding the fresh, crisp linens that somehow he knew that she was lovely. She was very pretty, but that was not why, for it was a beauty that he could not comprehend. She was thin, but not as thin as he was, and she was strong; it was strange, for she was stronger than the strength in her body and lovelier than a face could be. Suddenly he was glad that she was his mother, so happy that he jumped in the air and shouted as though Christmas had come.

"For Heaven sakes," she said, "what's come over you?" But he could not tell her; he could only beam upon her in his warmest fashion.

"Now if you could only shake your head, like this," she said, making a puffed-up face, "you'd be the image of your father."

"Mom," he said, his feet once more on the earth, "let's go to the show, Mom . . . I'll be the gentleman and you be the lady . . .

"And," he added, importantly, "we'll step out!"

"Step out? Where did you hear that?"

"Oh, people step out," he explained.

And his mother agreed, they would go, and gathered him into her arms.

They were pretending they were stepping out

when they left the house. She gave him the key to
the front door, impressing him with its tremendous
importance, because if he lost it, she said, they
would have to sleep in a tree. Mark carefully placed
it in his pocket; a moment later, he felt down in his
pocket frantically, to make sure it was still there.
They hurried toward the town.

It was thrilling to be out in the evening. Many
people were out walking then. The dredgermen and
their families usually came to town in the evening,
either to see the motion picture or to buy ice-cream
sodas in the Rose Confectionary. You could see them
strolling in from the highway, in groups, with the
men walking ahead of the women and talking re-
spectfully to each other, as workingmen will when
their work is done. Their children ran ahead, calling to each other, sometimes running arm in arm,
as fast as they could go.

In the evening when they came to town, the
dredgermen all wore blue-serge suits; and it seemed
that none of the suits ever fitted. Mark thought that
suits were not meant for their kind of bodies, but his
mother said that was not true. "You're used to seeing them working," she explained.

Those of the dredgermen who were young and
unmarried went to the saloon on the corner. Mark
knew the sound of their heavy shoes on the board
sidewalk and the squeak of the saloon door as it
closed behind them, shutting out the bright noises
and the light. The sight and the sound were strong

enough in his memory that they brought back a scene he could not remember seeing. But it was one summertime when he was out walking with his mother and father. Everyone had nodded to them and his father was tipping his hat, but still it was not a cheerful time, perhaps because the dark was there and the only light was overhead and down the street, the sundown on the red bricks of the buildings. Supper was over and the dredgermen were walking up the road, their white socks showing between their shoe tops and their trouser cuffs; their faces were rubbed red from washing. Some of the men were singing; and behind them their wives came walking in dark dresses that barely hung above the ground, wearing huge hats too gay for wan faces.

But now it was winter. Summer was a long time ago. He was walking along with his mother, holding her hand, but when he remembered those huge, frightening hats, he shivered. And someone was singing now, someone in the brick building across the street. He knew the song. "That's the Long, Long Trail A-windin'," he told his mother. "No," she replied, "that's 'Dardenella'." And when she spoke, he remembered the women again, walking slowly as though out of time, like dark people who moved toward him in his sleep. Mark took a good hold of his mother's hand, forgetting that in his pocket he had the key.

He was very glad when they reached the theater; the million lights in front of it lit up the ground for yards around. Almost everyone in town, he imagined, must be here; at least, everyone from school was here. He spied Judith and her mother just as they went in the door.

"Look," he shouted, "there's Mrs. Blake and Judith!"

"Shush," his mother replied; Mark looked up to find out why, but she wasn't looking at him . . . He hoped that she would remember that he liked to sit down in front with the fellows from school.

His mother pressed a silver dollar into his hand. "If you're the gentleman," she said, "you can buy the tickets." He strode to the ticket window, as casually as he could. He cleared his throat. "Two tickets, please. Two tickets for the lower floor," he said, with an important air.

The man inside the booth took his dollar and gave him back some ten-cent pieces. Mark gathered them into his hand and began counting them carefully. The man coughed. "If you don't mind, Sonny," he said; and Mark glanced at him to see what he meant, and then Mark started in at the beginning, counting his change over again.

Then, before he could finish, he felt his mother's hand on his shoulder; she was smiling at the people waiting behind him. "Come on, Dear," she said, in a sweeter tone than she usually used.

Mark followed her, but protested. "I was counting the change," he hissed.

"Just give it to me, Dear."

"But you said always to count my change." The people were looking at him, she said. Mark looked around, but everyone seemed busy. "I was just counting the change," he said, again.

"Yes, but you were keeping people waiting." Mark understood what that meant, for it was unpardonable to keep people waiting.

The motion-picture theater was really an old opera house, a heavy, thick place, with a balcony in the back which bulged out toward the stage like the fancy vest of a fat man. His mother found a seat next to Mrs. Perkins, whose husband worked for Mr. Needham, who was an old man with a cane. Mark looked around, but the old man was not there.

"You can go down front," his mother told him, "if you won't say a word during the performance." That was what he wanted to hear. He started to skip down the aisle, but remembered just in time that people might see him.

The difference between the lower floor and the seats down front was that there was a two-foot drop from one to the other. The children sat down there on benches, while the adults were in the back of the house, on opera plush, a red coarse material that tickled Mark's hands; the sight of it could run a shiver down his backbone. The chairs in the back were individual, but the fellows said that the couples who were "sticky" overcame that; they said that if you sneaked around after the lights were out you could see heads together and fingers interlaced on the arm rests.

Down front was the exciting place, just the same. Down here the older fellows threw peanut shells at the pianist, but the dark was so helpful they were never caught. No parent ever knew for sure if his child threw a peanut shell and everyone blamed some boys who were called ruffians, for ruffians came to the theater unaccompanied by their parents. "I don't know what some people think of," Mrs. Perkins had said, "letting their children run wild in the night." Oh, it was a pretty tough section down front, where Mark sat with all the hard-boiled fourth and fifth graders. It was no place for Judith; or for any girl, for that matter; no place for sissies, either, although it was under almost constant surveillance. Ushers, young ladies from the high school, prowled nervously up and down the aisles, searching for ruffians.

Most of the applause came from down front; that was also where the feet were stamped. When the time came, before the performance began, for the manager of the theater to step on the stage to introduce the men of the service, who attended in uniform—that was the time for applause; and the boys down front cheered the loudest. Mark joined in three hurrahs, one after another, for the soldier boys; and when the soldier boys stood up, shuffling and beaming, he beat his hands together and thought of his father, who had a uniform, too.

The fellows down front identified themselves with the characters in the serials and each week attended in suspense to learn whether the particular character in the film that they pretended to be had survived the fire or evaded the flood of the Friday before; and besides, it was necessary to know what predicament they would be in for the duration of next week.

Mark was unable to comprehend the serials completely, but he realized they were as exasperating as they were exciting, for he found that as a rule he played the hero, and the hero had to get into most of the difficulty. Unable as he was to read very well the titles in between the scenes, he worked out the plot for himself, maintaining in his mind a running conversation of the work of hero and villain, what had happened a moment ago and what would happen next. The time he had sat with his mother, he kept asking her questions; but she had whispered to him to keep quiet.

Down front he could not ask a single question. These fellows could all read. If he asked a question, they would think he was just a kid, and ignore him for the rest of his life. Yet, even though he asked no questions, they seemed to give him no attention. They did not even ask him if he would care to throw a peanut shell, for what he did they did not care. Ted Brown, for one, would not even speak to him because he was only in the first grade, for Ted Brown was a hero. He was the best baseball pitcher in the school; indeed, people said that when he grew older he would pitch as well as Olaf, Christina's son, who was in the high school. Like Olaf, he chewed. That became common knowledge one day when Ted was in the Fifth Grade, for the teacher had passed a law that no one was to chew gum in class, but that very afternoon she noticed that Ted Brown's jaws were moving up and down. With her ruler in her hand, she went down the aisle after him. "Spit it out!" she said, holding out her hand; and Ted did. But when she held out her hand, she did not realize that it was going to be tobacco.

Mark realized that he would be marked with honor if Ted Brown, the pitcher and tobacco-chewer, had spoken to him. But he did not; and Mark was reluctant to speak to him first. He was still turning over in his mind the advisability of speaking, when the lights in the house were turned off and the screen became bright for the motion picture.

First there was a serial with cowboys and horses —one white horse and five black ones; but almost before it began; the serial was done. An American flag appeared on the screen, and everyone cheered. Then the picture of the evening began. It was very exciting. An American ship had been sunk by a torpedo from a German submarine. Somehow, before the ship washed under the waves, an American girl and a gallant Navy officer were brought aboard the submarine. Some soldiers were taken aboard, too;

but they were angry; they waved their hands and protested against the sinking of their boat. So the German captain stepped forward and pointed a pistol at their heads. He shot them, one by one. You did not see them shot; you just saw his pistol flare and his smile to his friends, some more Germans who leered at him in frank admiration.

Mark himself had felt an occasional chill, but he was enjoying himself. The theater was dark and hushed; he could hear only the drone of the machine in the back of the theater; sometimes, though, in the exciting places, he heard behind him a great gasp, for then, like a wave, a shudder ran over the audience.

This motion picture was unlike the other two he had seen, except that the German officer had those funny intentions toward the American girl; he guessed that these intentions, all of them confusing, were in all the pictures. He had asked Judith what they meant, but all she knew was that the man in each case wished to kiss the woman; but that, she explained, women would always faint rather than be kissed. "That's one kind of kiss," she had told him. "There is another kind, and that is the kind that ends the story. The man wants to kiss the lady, and as soon as he does—that is the end of the story." Mark could not see any sense in that; personally, he liked pictures when cowboys rode horses and shot pistols.

Although it was not very clear, Mark could see

now that this German was carefully beginning some strategy to kiss the girl. Mark hoped hard that he would fail; and his hope must have been enough, for the German did fail. He tried to kiss her, again and again, but each time she repulsed him and told him to get away, you Beast. Once, when he got the pretty woman in the corner, she screamed and another German came running. But all he did was look at them and wink. A very evil wink, it was; and Mark realized it for a bad sign.

The captain was a very bad-looking man with a small mustache and big teeth. He had a scar on his cheek, and now and then he stroked it—and that was still another bad sign. For it seemed that the German, after such irritating frustration, could remain kissless no longer. He paced the submarine restlessly, head down and glancing from left to right; he was desperate. That was easy to see. And then it was that Mark heard a gasp from the audience; why, he did not know, until one of the fellows sitting behind him hissed, "He's going to skin her alive! . . . No—he's going to skin the sailor alive!"

And that is what he was going to do. Mark saw him sharpen a long, thin knife and make gestures to his friends; then they all walked over to the torpedo cylinder, and his friends gathered around him, as he pointed this way and that, discharging his instructions. "Jeez!" the boy behind Mark said aloud, "he's going to shoot 'em out through the torpedo chute!" Mark stared at the screen; he could see the

Germans laughing and slapping each other on the back, delighted with a punishment so novel.

Mark became very excited, and as scared as could be; he held his hands together and almost forgot to breathe. He saw the brave Navy officer, pacing up and down his cell, his hands handcuffed behind his back. Mark saw the pretty woman, determination upon her face, tied to her bed and praying to God with a gag in her mouth. Mark scarcely knew what to do. The Germans were going to *skin them alive!*

But fortunately for Mark, he felt at that moment a hand upon his shoulder. He looked up, shocked . . . but it was only his mother. He was certainly glad to see her. "Mark," she whispered. "Mark— close your eyes."

Should he do that, Mark wondered. He did not want to close his eyes; and yet he did want to close them, in a way. He wanted to see his mother's face, but the theater was too dark, so he closed his eyes; he closed them very tightly.

Mark opened his eyes once, but he thought he had better not look, and closed them again. He could feel the other fellows shivering with excitement. Oh, the ignominy of it!

After a long moment the piano player began playing loud and cheerfully, and Mark opened his eyes. His mother had gone back to her seat, and he saw on the screen that the pretty woman was still alive and that the American officer was kissing her. Everyone was aboard a battleship, the cringing German was kicked in the face by a sailor, and the American flag was waving; the audience loudly applauded. The lights in the theater were turned up then and the show was over. It was an exciting evening in the theater in 1918.

Mark turned to the boy behind him. "Didn't he skin her?" he asked. "No," said the boy, shortly.

As quickly as the crowd would let him, Mark scrambled up the aisle to his mother, who was standing with Mrs. Perkins waiting for him. "Did you keep your eyes closed?" she asked. She said that she did, too; and so had Mrs. Perkins. "You should have sat on the aisle," she told him, "where I could get you out."

She turned away from him to speak to Mrs. Perkins. "I knew I shouldn't have come," he heard her say, and as they talked on and on, he heard Mrs. Perkins say and repeat, and shake her head each time she said it, "I don't think movies like this are right. I don't, and I don't mind saying so."

Mark felt weak, as though he had not eaten, but for some reason he was eager to hear what Mrs. Perkins and his mother said. He edged around so that he got between them, away from the people who were moving up the aisle, but his mother moved him back into the aisle. "You go on up and wait for me in the lobby," she said. "I'll be right up."

"I want to stay with you," he told her.

"Go on up, Dear. I'll be along in just a moment."

He had to go; she squeezed his hand tenderly, but

he still had to go. He felt in his pocket to find if the key was still there, and it occurred to him that if he was the gentleman who brought the lady to the show, that she should not send him away.

In the lobby, where he stood thinking and trying to be stepped on less, he felt unaccountably sad. Once more he saw himself in the third person; he saw himself alone in the lobby, a stranger among all these people. He guessed that no one in the world cared about him. He moved over to look down the aisle, but she was still talking. He looked again and he suddenly saw a face that caused his heart to beat faster. He took a good look . . . It was that boy from the big house, who stood on the other side of the fence.

Mark watched him, warily. The boy was wearing different clothes and he was with his father and mother, but Mark knew him just the same, the sissy. Why, he hadn't even sat down in front with the fellows; he had sat with his *parents!* Watching him, Mark was both delighted and frightened, for without ever thinking about it, he knew exactly what he was going to do to that boy; and just before he did it, he knew it should not be done.

The boy, without seeing him, walked past; and Mark stepped out. "*Sissy!*" he said. Just that, a loud hiss; and no more.

But it was enough; everyone heard it. In his rage, Mark was completely confused, but he saw that from all sides, as in a dream, there was a sudden turning of heads; from all sides people were looking at him. The boy jumped and looked around in alarm, to back squarely between his parents.

What could have followed, Mark never knew, for his mother's hand was on his shoulder and she was propelling him forward. "You march straight out of here," he heard her saying, "March!" And when outside the cold air struck them, she pulled his coat closer around his shoulders and said, over and over again, "The idea! . . . The idea!"

And after a moment, she added that she was ashamed of him. Mark was sorry, but not very sorry. All the way home, and it was a long way, he was fairly happy. Everyone had paid attention to him.

Eleventh Chapter

BUT MARK did not receive from his contemporaries the sudden admiration he expected. Gratitude and praise, for that matter, had never come his way; and their tardiness caused him some reflection. He realized that he had with great courage disparaged that boy in the Opera House. It compared in stature to the hard-boiled work of some big fellow. Yet, the act failed to bring him much renown. He had done more than his part by telling the story in detail to every boy that he respected, and some would listen and some would not. It did seem to him that his heroism was given a callous indifference. Somehow he had been deprived of an acknowledgement he had earned. He felt forlorn and cheated, and he felt that way all through one Thursday afternoon lesson in Literature; and when school was over at last, he strolled home in deep meditation, concerned with the fact that James Russell Lowell was an American poet, born in Massachusetts, and that no matter what poor Mark did, no crowd would hail him.

There was one part of the story that he did not emphasize; he did not stress that grown-ups had been present when the insult occurred. Even when he thought of the grown-ups or remembered their quick alarm, he felt in himself a flutter of misgiving. More than once he had deeply regretted that his enemy's parents had been present that evening, for if adults had any part in it, the incident was not important. Parents naturally were unable to understand that the disagreement of children was no concern of theirs. Had the situation been reversed, had his parents been angry at the boy's parents, he would have left them alone. But adults could not understand that they should retain their lofty and secure position, to let him and his enemy be.

Still, he was rather happy to think of how that sissy had jumped between his parents; and of how, in the beginning, that sissy had leered through the fence at him, and how, too, with great dexterity, he had secured his revenge. And, in a way, it was nice to recall how shocked everyone had been, comforting to feel upon him again the attention he had for the moment commanded.

However, it had made his mother unhappy; that was the worst of it. And she had said that she would have to write a letter to his father about it. She really should overlook it. Yet, she wouldn't because no matter how frankly he talked to her, she still believed the insult was partly for her. Parents couldn't get things straight somehow.

Mark was still too young to consider if the insult to the boy had been worth the subsequent bother. All he knew was that in the schoolyard none of the heroes praised him for having acted in such a brave manner. They failed to recognize emulation. But even when he was being punished for his action of that evening; even when his mother sent him to apologize to his enemy, even the moment he faced his enemy's parents, he knew in himself a small glow of satisfaction. And it is true that if the boy's mother had not patted his head, he would not have cried at all.

Mark never settled the problem and in time he forgot all of that evening except its satisfaction. It was simply one attempt he had taken to be like the older fellows, and it was but an obvious effort among many others more subtle. He decided that boys older than himself lived a smoother life; their days followed one another with order and dignity. He, too, must be calm. The older fellows did not wish him to run to them and shout whenever he thought of a good idea. They wished to be approached with respect and it was now his ambition to please them.

That ambition came to Mark in an unusual manner, through a conversation he had one day with Mr. Anderson.

On a Saturday morning Richard and he went to

pick holly berries behind Mr. Anderson's farm. The month was October, and Christmas was a long way off yet, but it was coming closer because the first holly had appeared.

When Richard whistled out front for him, Mark was not quite ready. He heard his mother ask Richard if he would come in and have a cup of chocolate while he was waiting, but Richard replied that he guessed he would just wait outside. Mark came upon him sitting on the back step. "Hello," he said. "Hello," Richard replied, and they looked at one another not unkindly.

Mark's mother dashed out to them, casting smiles and good will in both directions, saying that she would accompany them if they wished. Richard looked uneasy; it was Mark's place to reply, and he hastily told her they would be all right. She said no more about it, and he was glad, for if she came with them, there would be no adventure; the trip would be as prosaic as walking to the store. The woods would retain no mystery and the holly would not lurk in the hidden places.

His mother then wondered if he should bring a coat, to wear over his sweater in case the afternoon became cold. "Richard hasn't one," he told her; but Richard, she said, wore a heavier sweater. Mark was suddenly petulant; he was *not* going to wear a coat. She ran back in the house and returned with his heavy blue sweater. Mark slipped it on and turned to Richard. "See how good it is," he said. But Richard only pointed to his own sweater. "Mine's *red,*" he replied, and showed it to both of them.

Although the day was not warm, the sun felt warm on Mark's back when he started, and it got in his eyes when he turned to wave back at his mother and hear again her cautions to be careful. "Why don't you wave?" he asked, but Richard replied, "She's not my mother, so I don't have to." There was so much logic in that statement that Mark turned his mind from it and began to think of something else.

When they passed Mr. Anderson's farm, the ground rose abruptly; they were forbidden to go on toward the mountain, but they could search here, in the pine woods, for the holly.

Both Mark and Richard must have been wary in their conversation; certainly they did not mention that Saturday in the kitchen or the man who wanted bulrushes, but whether they mentioned anything else, either, is doubtful. They simply walked along, occasionally running one ahead of the other, saying little, but pointing things out to each other in a courteous fashion, becoming warm and cold by turn, as their trail led into the shade of the pine trees and beyond it.

Their destination was a great rock, smooth and gray; and when they reached it, both boys paused for breath. From the top of the rock they could see Mark's house, almost a mile away; they could even see the town, far down below. Richard said he could also see the railroad station, but Mark knew he lied, for the stores and warehouse hid it.

The holly grew on the other side of the rock, and they were the best berries in the world, much larger and redder than common, ordinary berries you could buy at Christmas time; but the bushes were small, more of a black than a green, and tucked into nooks between mounds of dying rock, for there age and the seasons had crumbled the rocks enough so that soil stayed there from the wind, in the sheltered corners where the holly took root.

Mark wanted to find the berries before Richard did. But they both had skinned their knees, scrambling over rocks, before Mark saw the first bunch. He began a whoop to Richard, but paused for some reason he did not know; he looked about the quiet, shaded glen, and the tall trees overhead, and then called softly to Richard, motioning him to come. Richard thought something was wrong, and stole over, suspecting a wild animal behind every rock. Without a word, Mark pointed out the berries.

They were busy picking and had almost overcome the quiet of the place, when Richard stopped, as though he was tired. "I think I'll climb up on the rock again," he said; but instead he came over close to Mark and looked at his berries. "Have you got enough?" he asked, and when Mark looked around, left and right, and nodded, Richard again suggested they should climb to the rock.

"It's kinda quiet in here," he said.

"No wild animals here, though," Mark replied.

"No sir!" Richard said, loudly, "no wild animals in here!" And again they both looked around. The glen was very quiet, green and fragrant even in October. The ground was damp; the rocks were white from the wash of the rains, and the trees rose like a cathedral to cover the sky. Down in the grasses something stirred.

"Lizard," Richard explained, and Mark nodded.

"That's all that's in here," Richard said, but Mark was not so sure. He listened.

"That's all they got in here," Richard repeated. "Isn't it, Mark?"

Almost in a whisper, Mark said: "There could be something else in here." And he listened again. He heard nothing, but the glen came about him, closer and closer, as though each time he turned to Richard, the glen came one step nearer. He looked at the trees, to see their identity, for the face of the rock, for something alive and green. And now he felt a secret thrill.

"Richard," he said, after a moment. "Richard, there's *something* else in here."

Richard laughed, and quickly moved a step away. "Have you got enough holly?" he said, and when Mark did not reply, he asked the question again; but he was already walking away.

"Let's go," he whispered, and walked the faster. Then, when he saw that Mark was coming, he cried, "Let's get out of this place!" He started to run; and when he heard Mark running, too, he ran as rapidly as he could. But Mark, more thrilled than he was frightened, easily passed him, darted through the woods, and came out in the clearing near Mr. Anderson's place, and at last into the bright daylight. He hesitated, then slipped through the fence; he would have run on home, had he not seen his old friend Mr. Anderson. He was so glad to see him that he ran up to his porch, breathlessly.

"See my holly!" he cried.

The holly had become something precious; he had taken it from the glen. He had stolen it and carried it away from that glen; and now, green and red, and harsh in his hand, it was a mutilated head from a room in the giant's house.

Mr. Anderson stepped down from the porch, and smiled. "Slow up," he said. "You're like a wild Indian."

Richard came running up likewise out of breath, but he still clutched his holly. His flight, though, had shaken off most of the berries. "But that's all right," Mr. Anderson told him, "there'll be a lot more of it later in the season."

"We've been out behind the rock," Mark said.

"So I see," Mr. Anderson replied. "And you had a race back?" he suggested. "And now you're winded."

"I don't want to go home yet," Richard said. "I guess I'll just sit here." He laid down his holly and wiped his face in his sleeve.

"That's right, just rest a bit," Mr. Anderson told them. "But come on into my house and we'll scrape up a snack to eat while you're resting."

Mark had never been in Mr. Anderson's house before, but he had often wondered what it looked like inside, for the outside looked so different from any other house that he imagined the interior must be equally different. Somehow he had imagined it as one large, gray room, not unlike a cave. But he was wrong. There were rooms the same as anywhere else.

Mark glanced around, curious to see everything; they were in the kitchen, a long room with a plump stove at one end. Pans hung down from the wall, and on the table there was an oilcloth cover, so faded and worn that the finish was gone in many places, revealing the white cheesecloth underneath. The wood floor was bare, and wear through the years had left it uneven. The room was like Mr. Anderson, Mark thought, for it was rough and scrubbed looking, and brown with age.

"Just make yourself to home," Mr. Anderson told them, for both boys were standing uncertainly in the middle of the floor.

Mark watched Mr. Anderson remove his hat and place it on a rack that already held the brown overcoat he knew so well. Richard followed after, putting his cap on the rack, but Mark stuffed his in a pocket.

Mr. Anderson was wearing a dark flannel shirt,

buttoned to the neck, but he had no tie. It occurred to Mark that perhaps he did not have to, because of his beard. Mark watched him as he slowly rolled up his sleeves, filled a basin with water, and washed his hands.

It was fascinating, seeing him do all this; he was like no other person Mark had ever seen. He looked broad and angular, without his coat; his wrists were large and brown, but his arms were pale above them. His elbows made knobs in his sleeves and his shoulders were sharp. Mark thought he looked like a tree, but he did not tell him so.

Richard must have been as fascinated, particularly with Mr. Anderson's beard, for Mark heard him asking, "Why do you wear whiskers, Mr. Anderson?" And Mark was embarrassed; this was not the kind of question to ask.

But Mr. Anderson laughed. "I dunno exactly." He dried his hands and felt his beard tentatively. "Guess I just about always have had it, 'cept when I was a young one and showed off by shaving." He laughed again. "I had a kind of razor I'll bet you never saw—a straight razor. Swedish steel, it was, and when I was a boy I wouldn't have swapped it for a house and lot."

And after a pause, he added, "I guess, anyway, that when I first came West there wasn't time or place much to get rid of whiskers."

"Does it take long to grow them?" Richard asked, leaning closer, for a better look.

"Pretty long," Mr. Anderson replied. "Pretty long, all right . . . Only you don't put your mind to it, so you don't notice how long it takes." He laughed at that.

"I remember," he continued, "that when I was a young one about your age I used to look at my daddy's beard and wonder why I didn't have one. You see, my mother wasn't living then, and I lived out in the Illinois country with my father and my brothers—and they all had beards!" He laughed again, and this time Mark joined in, only he did not know what there was to laugh about. But it was impolite not to laugh when others did.

Mr. Anderson said, "You boys go into the parlor and sit down an' I'll rustle up a snack." Both Mark and Richard hesitated. "Right in there," he said, pointing to the door. "We'd better hurry it up, I guess, for you boys'll have to be getting on home pretty soon . . . But I don't have many people for dinner," he said, "and I'll just be a moment."

Richard paused on the threshold and wiped his feet, for the parlor was a different kind of a place than the kitchen. To Mark the room seemed a faded pink. The chairs and sofa had pink felt cushions and a lamp on the stone-top table had a pink and wobbly shade. It seemed close in here, but perhaps he was warm from having run so far. His sweater became unbearable; he felt sure it would stifle him. He slipped out of it as fast as he could, but then he was uncertain of what he should do with it. It would be impolite just to put it on a chair. He placed it across the back of a chair, at first, to see how it would look, but changed his mind and carried it to the kitchen and hung it on the coat rack.

When lunch was ready, Mr. Anderson said, "I haven't any cookies, boys, but I've got plenty of fresh milk . . . and I've spread the butter thick on the bread." He looked from one to the other.

"I sure liked butter when I was a boy," he added, and both Richard and Mark exclaimed that they liked it, too. Only it was wrong to eat so much butter, for when you ate butter at home you took it away from some soldier boy in France. But Mark did not tell his host that.

"Pitch in, boys," Mr. Anderson said. "Plenty of everything."

Mark felt awkward, at first; he was not sure he should be eating at Mr. Anderson's house. From the side of his eyes he watched Richard disapprovingly, for Richard had forgotten to wash his hands and they were still stained from the holly berries.

After lunch Mr. Anderson showed them something he had in the parlor. He had to raise the curtains first. "I'm not in here much myself," he explained. "I said I'm not here much. Always said the parlor was the ladies' room. Always used to tell my wife that. Guess the parlor don't get the curtains raised from one day to the next."

Mr. Anderson reached into a cabinet and brought out a small, brown box; he blew the dust from it.

"Guess you never saw anything like this before," he said, and held it up to the light. "Did you, now?"

They both examined it. "It's a cigarette case," Richard said, "only nicer."

"Nope, it looks like that all right, but you got to guess again." Mark thought and thought, but it was just a box for holding things, as close as he could tell. "It's a cuff-link box," he guessed, after a moment.

"Well," Mr. Anderson replied, "I guess I'll have to tell you . . . It's a music box. Look!" And he turned a key in it and set the box down on the table. A tune came from it, faint and tinkling, as though from a great distance.

Mr. Anderson looked from one boy to the other. "Well," he said, "what do you think of it? Isn't that pretty fine?"

"What's it for?" Richard asked. He picked it up, to look underneath the lid.

Mr. Anderson took it from him. "Just a little music, son." He put it back in the cabinet. "Just a little music."

"Have you got a phonograph?" Richard asked. "I don't see a phonograph."

"No, this is all," Mr. Anderson told him. "I just thought you'd like to hear it."

"Where did you get it?" Mark asked, for he had never seen anything like it before.

"It belonged to my wife," Mr. Anderson replied. "Would you like to hear it again?"

Mark said that he would, and Mr. Anderson took it from the cabinet and played the distant tune again.

"Where did she get it?" Mark inquired, and immediately Mr. Anderson began to smile. "Nowhere around here. We brought it West with us, and it's very old. Used to belong to her mother, so it's very old . . . older than either one of you, older than me." He looked at them in surprise. "Why it is," he said, "it's older than the West—older than all this, the town and all!" He looked at the boys and nodded his head.

"Huh!" said Richard, "I'll bet you're kidding!"

Mr. Anderson said, "Don't be too sure of that. Neither one of you'd known the town if you'd seen it then. The Blakes and us were just about the first folks here—but I was here before them with the Carter boys. That was before I went East to get married."

"You mean Mr. Blake?" Mark asked, thinking of his friend.

Mr. Anderson thought that was a good joke. "No, Mark, I mean his daddy. James Blake was hardly born yet . . . No, I guess I'm wrong there. He was just a boy about your age, though, because old man Blake came out here the year after he was married." He hesitated, running his finger slowly over the smooth top of the music box. "The sons didn't take after their fathers," he said. "They didn't take after their fathers at all."

Richard had walked over to the parlor table and with one finger was idly touching the lamp shade. Mark was politely listening to Mr. Anderson.

"Sit down, Mark, make yourself at home," Mr. Anderson said, and sat down himself. Mark sat across from him, and Richard slumped into the sofa.

"I guess I'm an old one all right," he heard him say. "I said I'm an old one—but not as old as you'd think. I'll be sixty-three come April, but I was married when lads these days start high school.

"Why, Mark," he said, "I remember your mother when she was no higher than you—and neither was James Blake. And a pretty little thing, she was, too —but shy. A fine one, but you couldn't get within fifty feet of her . . . You just ask her sometime if she remembers when she used to climb in the poplar tree by the old Blake house. She could climb a tree faster than any of them. Climb like greased lightning. Used to run and hide when the visitors come." Mr. Anderson paused, and leaned back in his chair. "You wouldn't know the town," he said. "You wouldn't know the town."

He looked again at Mark and chuckled. "Mark, I remember her wedding in the old Blake house— when she married your daddy. I guess you can't remember then, can you? Eh?" He winked at Richard, for Mark had failed to see the joke, and tried to remember.

A long time ago he had heard his mother telling of living in the old Blake place, a large brown house, surrounded by trees, so that it was almost a castle; but he was not sure what his mother had said. He only half-remembered; and, besides, it was difficult to think of her as living anywhere else than in his house.

"Places change all the time, Mark," he heard Mr. Anderson saying. "Everything's always moving. Take this town—it's changed so much that if you had seen it then you wouldn't know it now. The world's always changing, so that pretty soon it won't be as it is now, any more than it will be the same again as when I came just after my marriage."

Mr. Anderson stopped for a moment and filled his pipe. "I don't want to talk your leg off, boys, but when I saw you today I began thinking of how things changed and how much they would change. The war changes the world, all right, but it'd change anyway. They say it's about over now, but I don't think it'll end so easy. I just thought when I saw you today that I hope you won't have to live it down." Mr. Anderson looked at them crossly. "I said I hope you won't have to live it down," he repeated, "I'd hate to think of you living in something we started."

Mark did not understand what his friend was saying, and his face must have revealed his confusion, because Mr. Anderson said, "I don't blame you, Mark. Guess I don't make myself clear. I've got a thick tongue, Mark. Always had it . . . Be careful you learn how to speak, Mark. Don't have a thick tongue."

Richard asked what a thick tongue was, and Mr. Anderson told him it was something that got in your way when you tried to say what you thought; and Richard nodded to show that he understood.

Mr. Anderson took a large watch from his pocket and then looked at the boys. "Guess I better send you packing," he said. "Don't want your mothers to get worried."

Richard jumped to his feet and thanked Mr. Anderson for his lunch. "That's all right, you don't have to thank me," Mr. Anderson told him.

Mark saw him look around the room. "I wish I had some toys or marbles around," he heard him saying. "I'd like to give you boys something to carry away with you. Don't like my guests to go 'way empty-handed." He looked at Mark and winked, and Mark felt happy.

Mr. Anderson walked with them to the porch, and then followed them across the yard to the stile. He gave Richard a boost over and then helped Mark. He leaned against the fence, puffing his pipe. "I'll tell you what, boys, I can't give you anything to take along with you—but come back in twenty years and I'll show you a new world. You can have it for your own, and put a fence around it."

"Really!" Mark said, impulsively; and Mr. Anderson smiled.

"Sure," he said, "you'll grow right into it. Twenty years," he repeated, "don't forget."

"You're kidding," Richard said. "Aren't you kidding us?"

Mr. Anderson said, "I may be and I may not. I'm not sayin' . . . But come back and see for yourself. Come back sooner than that. Come back and see me whenever you like."

After he had walked away with Richard, Mark turned to look at his friend. He was still leaning against the fence, his long arms resting on the top rail; and when he saw Mark turn, he waved. So Mark waved back at Mr. Anderson, as if to thank him for the world.

That conversation was not forgotten, for even as he built his age with incidents of the day, like a child piling blocks for a stairway, so Mark remembered that afternoon in Mr. Anderson's house as a step toward becoming an older fellow. Now, more than anything else, he wished to be older. He wished he could grow up right away into this world he had been promised.

Mark had a long talk with his mother about it. He had asked her, to begin with, what she would do when they arose on the morning of February Eleventh.

"I'm going to spank you eight times," she said, "and then I'll give you one more to grow on."

"And what else?"

"Oh, I may give you a present—if you're a good boy."

Mark reminded his mother that he was a good boy, a fairly good boy, as Mr. Anderson had said. He paused to consider what present he would like the best of all, and he finally decided upon an army tank—a brown and red one, like the army tank in the store window. They were exactly like real army tanks, although smaller, of course. And when he had it he would be eight years old.

"When I'm in the second grade," he said to his mother, "I'll be eight years old, won't I?"

He saw her counting the months on her fingers.

"Won't I?" He demanded to know.

"Do you want to be?" she asked.

Indeed! He glowed with the thought.

"Well, then," she said, "you will be."

"You know," he said, as though a great truth had of a sudden been revealed to him, "I think I like to hear people talk."

"Don't tell me," she replied, "you're all ears."

"That's because I'm growing up, liking to hear people talk so much." He considered this a startling conclusion, but his mother was not even amazed enough to look up from the bed she was making.

"When I grow older and older," he told her, "I'll love you more and more . . . And when Daddy and you are old, I'll keep good care of you—and buy you presents!"

"Ah!" she replied, "Brave words," and smiled at

him. Now Mark was filled with great, warm thoughts. How much he would do for them, and how they would admire him! With what joy they would say he was a fine, big man! "I'll be a man!" he shouted, for he suddenly saw himself, in a dazzling revelation, as a man in an overcoat, with a great black cane. Until then he had always imagined himself as an older boy, but never as a man. It was as completely radiant a triumph as the time he first struggled from the floor to stand alone on his legs.

"When I am in the second grade," he said, slowly, descending to the earth again. "When I am in the second grade . . ."

"You'll want to be in the third," his mother told him.

And she added, "Please don't age too rapidly."

"Then do you think," he asked, "that the older fellows will like to have me play with them?"

But she said that he must not try too hard to be like older boys. He must play with children his own age. "The important thing," she said, "is to be sure and have Richard and Judith, and children your own age like you, for they're the ones you will have to live with." She reminded him of what Mr. Anderson had said. "That's what he meant by a world of your own."

It may have been then, or sometime after, that his mother told him the story of the crooked apple tree, an obscure and tantalizing story that was supposed to help him adjust himself to the boys and girls at school. She said he must feel as comfortable with them as he did at home. "Some boys have sisters and brothers to play with," she told him, "but you will be an only child."

Mark always knew the crooked tree was a special one, living out in the wind; but until his mother told him the story, he did not know that it was like the world. In the winter it was dry and hard, she said, with its bark protecting it from the cold, but in the spring new life came to it. The tree became green and prepared blossoms for April; and in September the tree bore its apples.

His mother said that even in winter the tree had a promise for April; and that even when it was in blossom, the tree knew winter was coming. The world had seasons just like that. When she was a little girl, the world seemed like a very fine place, for it was in blossom. The trunk was badly bent, but neither she, nor his father, nor the wisest man on earth knew it, because the blossoms were so beautiful.

But when the world was like that then, all white and pink, no one knew that after spring there had to be fall. "People in the world were ever so polite to each other, for they lived an easy life." That spring was a time of gentle breezes and of skies as blue as lake water. The people who came into the world then thought that season would always be.

These people would never be like him. They were bent with the tree too far one way. "They were cramped; they laced up their minds as well as their clothes, as though to enclose themselves from life." You could tell how they were from their homes.

"They filled their houses with furniture and crowded the corners with knick knacks. Pictures and books had to be put behind glass and decorations had to be on everything. Pianos had to have vases on them; tables had to have scarfs and centrepieces, to make them pretty. The wood was not enough, you see."

If he were not his father's son, he would not know what death was, until one saw he saw it and became frightened. Even the word was avoided, because things that were vital were too dangerous to mention. Just the same, in the spring the old bark is pushed away by the new life within the tree.

But he would·be different, she said, for his world began in the fall. He would know that winter followed. He was born to make a world that would one day fit him, but not his parents. It would not be his world alone, for it would belong to all the children his age now. "There's not as much connection between you and me," she said, "as there will be between you and Richard or Judith," for there was a dampness in grown-up people, but in little children the sunlight was direct. She made a picture for him, and it was so funny that he laughed with delight. He was a villain, a comical villain that looked like a puppydog, as he got ready to tear up the pink ribbons.

Now in the tree the season was fall, and winter would be next; but he would be all right because he would be ready for it. "The world will change and maybe you will change it; and before long, before many months, now that you have started to school, there will be a conflict between you and me; and you will be right and I shall be right, for one generation will not know another." But if he loved her, if he loved his father, he need not fear. He must remember that.

That was the story. Mark could not understand it, but he remembered it. The tree became vastly important. The way it grew apples was the way children grew up. His mother said the apples had seeds to grow more trees, but when he opened a fallen apple, he saw it was rotten inside like the soft white stuff under an overturned stone. He decided that when the tree dropped the apples it did an awful thing.

But if his mother talked to him this way, then he was really growing up. He could not tell if he was any larger, or longer, for that matter; but some nights he had aches in his legs. And the dentist said he was going to get his adult teeth some day.

Early one morning, when his clothes were off, he stood on a chair and looked in the mirror; he felt his legs and the top of his head, and it was then that he decided he was surely growing up. That day he did not walk—he marched to school.

Twelfth Chapter

UNFORTUNATELY, JUDITH was feeling very happy that morning. She happened to be wearing a very nice dress and her mother had taken great care with her curls. At her desk in the classroom, where she sat as small as she could, a pale and fragile halo hung about her head, for goodness was in her, such radiant goodness that occasional impulses of delight roved warmly through her body; and more than once she could have hugged herself. Teacher had smiled at her sweetly and Judith wished that she could raise her hand now and tell Miss Matthews how much she loved her.

When Judith thought of love, she thought of her mother. How her dear mother loved her! Mother said that she just could not do without Judith, for she was a present from Heaven. How God must love her, too! How nice that God loved her and helped her with Arithmetic! Judith felt warm and wonderful all over as she applied herself to the problem in the book of how many hypothetical yeast cakes a girl named Barbara bought at the store for twenty-three cents. She carefully drew a design across the top of the paper, for the paper would look bare and selfish without it, and in the design she placed many beating hearts, and to each one she gave wings.

Someone in the class enquired if yeast cakes made bread. Of course they did; Judith felt sorry for that poor pupil who was so ignorant. There were pictures of yeast cakes in the book, yellow things that even looked like little loaves of bread. Judith studied them in detail; and, in a moment, the yeast cakes were real enough that she could have lifted them from the page to put them on her desk. She thought that it was a shame that she really could not, for she would take them to the poor people. She wondered if Barbara was poor, but the book had no picture of Barbara; still, when Judith closed her eyes, she could see her. She looked at Barbara very closely and felt sorry for her, because she did not have really nice curls. But Barbara was very sweet. She wished to kiss Barbara.

There was a low murmur of voices in the room and when Judith opened her eyes, she smiled to everyone, even to Peg, who had tried to put his twenty-three cents into yeast cakes and had failed. She gave an extra big smile to Mark, who was bent to his book, for he was her favorite and would some day become her husband, if she would have him.

Then, as sometimes happens, as calamities of the worse sort occasionally come from innocent beginnings; then, in that tender moment—the school-bell rang, a noise of steel, loud and sharp.

It was noontime; and now Mark was going to get into trouble, for as Judith left the room her eyes were still misty and her thoughts were vague and dear. She was seeing her mother and God, Arithmetic and Barbara. And then, from afar, she saw Mark. He floated near her, so she reached out and touched him; and it felt so wonderful to touch her old friend, that she stood on her tip-toes, her hands on his shoulders, impulsively to kiss him on the cheek.

Until then there had been noise; everyone had been breathing regularly. Friends had been talking to each other, and one boy had already started to run for his lunch pail. But movement ended and a sudden great hush came upon that schoolyard. The boy who had been running for his lunch, stopped; and his mouth dropped open in amazement. He left it that way. And from everyone who had been talking, came a long-drawn breath.

The moment held, and stretched, and finally broke; Mark stood still and thought he would die. He meant to glance quickly around, but there was no use doing that; everyone had seen her do it. He felt like closing his eyes, but even that movement failed him, for he had slumped into insensibility, somehow without falling down. But even as he waited for the wave to fall, he hoped that Judith realized what she had done, but Judith walked slowly away, and dread walked with her. Mark had to stand and face alone the hell he knew would be coming.

It was such a pity. He had been doing well until then, until Judith did this to him. But he might have known that sometime her impulsive demonstrations of love would get him into trouble. One day had peacefully followed another, with order and with dignity; autumn had turned to winter, and Christmas was coming. He would soon have been no different than anyone else and all the school would have been his friend. But now it was noontime and he was not hungry. Mark looked at the wave of oncoming faces, of eyes and teeth, and chins and shoulders; he looked, and didn't know what to do.

It was Richard who whooped the loudest—Richard, his old friend, who was first to take advantage.

"Hah!" Richard cried, with delight, from that wall of faces, "hah, hah!" And he looked from one boy to another, and in a moment they all were laughing.

Mark turned on Richard; he could not see clearly and a great beating was in his ears. Richard's face was the only one distinct among the many, and it was to him that he spoke. "What do you mean— *hah?*" But Richard, instead of saying he was sorry, once more turned to the others and grinned; and there arose a great chorus of hollers and whistles, even from the older fellows.

Mark wanted to jump into those faces and smash and kick them, but he realized this was an impossibility. Instead he stepped up to Richard and, in a petulant tone, said, "Keep still!" It was at that moment he decided that his predicament was entirely Richard's fault.

But Richard refused to admit it. He and Mark were suddenly surrounded with fellows; the girls who had been standing there a moment ago, were gone. They had to face each other, but Mark was not as angry now as he had been, for all the notoriety and confusion gave him a feeling of weakness; and he was looking at Richard in chagrin, for it should not be his old friend that he faced. He hoped that Richard would say he was sorry, but Richard seemed to draw confidence from the boys around him; he was defiant.

Peg had come up, grinning, making excited noises, with his chin wagging up and down above the red ruff of his heavy sweater; never before did his brown moles take such an evil turn. He stepped behind Mark and gave him a shove toward Richard. "Go ahead, tough guy," he said, "lick 'im!"

"He can't do it," Richard said, and doubled up his fists.

"That's the way," Peg told him. "Tell him." And turning to Mark, he added, "Go ahead, you're so tough."

"He's a-scared to," Richard explained; and everyone took the statement as a battle-cry. "Scared, scared." Mark heard the words, coming again and again from this circle of faces and sweaters and pushing elbows. The circle swayed back and forth, pushing in on him and then widening. Overhead the sun was high and the shade was cold; and Mark hoped something would happen, that even the sun would drop and in justice kill them all. "He's scared, scared," they were saying, shoving him with elbows one way and another.

He spoke for the first time. "I'm not scared," he said, in a thoughtful tone.

"Then why don't ya show him?" And Richard thrust out his chin. Mark considered hitting it.

"He can lick you," someone called.

"Sure I can," said Richard, "any old day."

"Huh!" Mark replied, in what he hoped sounded like disgust, for he realized he had to say something defiant.

And they continued to argue the matter until a place came in their assertions where proof was needed. Mark seemed less anxious than Richard to submit any kind of proof, but both murmured briefly of having on their good clothes. But Peg insisted that the matter be proven. If Richard said that he could lick Mark, and if Mark contended he could not; well, then he had to prove to Peg that he really could. And everyone agreed that it was so.

"You're afraid of him," Peg told Richard.

"Huh! I'm not afraid of that skinny guy."

"You are, too. Look at ya tremble! Turn around —you got yellow all down your back." Peg told him that, and Richard's chin began to tremble. Peg, sneering left and right, pretending to come over to Mark's side. "My chum wins," he explained. Richard looked at Mark as though he hated him.

It must have been at almost this minute that Mark realized that he and Richard had ceased to be friends, for it is not often true that defiant words and force end grudges, but that a wariness comes to proclaim itself friendship. Mark seemed to know that then, but it was not his concern so much as that he did not want to hurt Richard—and, more important, that he did not want to get hurt. But it seemed too late to stop now; they had to fight. Everyone else was determined.

Peg gave his new friend Mark a great shove toward Richard. "Get 'im," he said, "I know you can do it." But Mark hesitated, and in that moment Richard came at him. He struck out at Mark with both hands and bumped into him so hard that Mark fell back against the granite wall of the schoolhouse.

It felt funny, at first, trying to hit Richard's face. Mark was angry enough, because the wall had hurt his back, but his fists would not obey his mind; he could not hit Richard with his bare hands. With boxing gloves he would have been all right, but now his arms felt too light and his bare hands were too much a part of him to be weapons. He tried, but they would not obey; he could not hit Richard with them and there was no use trying.

Richard, though, was hitting him around the head and pushing him backward. Once, Mark lashed out in defense, but his fist did not go far enough. In return Richard hit him with both hands at once; and Mark grabbed him by the shoulders and shoved him away as hard as he could, so that Richard almost stumbled over backward.

There was a great shout from the circle around them. The wall of pushing faces dissolved in one place to let Richard fall. Everyone was yelling for Mark to hit him again, for he was off his balance; and Mark could have hit him, too, a pretty one, as everyone later said. But Mark had not his boxing gloves; he had to let Richard recover his balance.

And Richard came back at him rushing; Mark could see he was crying, and for no reason he knew, for Richard was no longer his friend, impulsive tears came to his own eyes, so that he could scarcely see. Richard's fists were hard; his knuckles hurt when they hit. He wanted to whisper to Richard; he wanted to whisper that they should wrestle. He tried to get hold of him again, but every time he grabbed at some part of his clothing, Richard hit himself loose.

"Sock him!" the fellows shouted; and Richard followed their brief advice.

The air was so cold that Mark's face was stinging, as though ice were against it. He tried to keep his

eyes open, but they were better closed. In his groping, he caught hold of Richard's arm and swung on
it until they both fell to the ground. He tried to hold
him down; they were both grunting and panting,
but the ground felt good, it was so smooth and cool.

Someone shouted a cat-call, and then all the boys
began to boo. Richard twisted harder than ever, to
roll himself loose. Getting to his feet, he swung
Mark's legs against the granite wall, so that while
he was standing up, Mark lay against the building,
feeling the throb in his knee.

"Get up—you're scared!" Richard said to him,
breathlessly; and his saying it was a knife in Mark's
heart, and suddenly Mark did not care what happened; all he wanted was to get away and never
come to school again. He wanted his mother, and he
wondered thickly if there was anyone in the world
who was his friend. He could tell without looking
that he had torn his stocking. What would his
mother say? And what *would* she say about his
fighting? That stayed in his mind as he wondered
if this fight would ever end. Every breath felt dry
and hard. But he was recovering his wind, and with
it his mind began to clear. His heart was beating as
large as before, but he was thinking better now.

And when he scrambled to his feet, he tried again
to catch hold of Richard; but he was thinking of
other things, so that even the blows seemed not as
hard as they had been. Richard was rushing in;
there was no expression on his face. He did not even

- 206 -

seem to see, as though he hit without looking. But Mark did not mind anymore. He was through with him, forever. And then, in a flash, Mark saw Peg's face. Peg was holding back the circle, his arms spread out; and now Mark knew at last what he would do.

Mark stumbled back from Richard and held up his hand, palm out, to stop him. "Wait!" he cried. "*Wait!*"

And as Richard hesitated, confused, as Mark intended him to be, he quickly stepped around him and walked up to Peg. His nose stung; he was sniffling, and his knee hurt. But, without a pause, he hit Peg right in the face, as hard as he could.

The blow no doubt was herculean, but it was not herculean enough, for Peg changed from bewilderment to pain, and finally to rage; and he rushed at Mark with a surprised roar, but Mark just closed his eyes, felt the blow heavy on his face, and stumbled back to the ground. Peg kicked him, but he did not mind.

The fight had become unfair. Everyone knew that; and, as Mark got warily to his feet, holding his bleeding nose in his hand, the janitor of the school, who could not be located until then, rushed in scolding and pushed Peg away.

Lengthy as it seemed to Mark, the fight had taken in all no more than a few minutes, but it lasted long enough, at that, to give him a reputation. He was hailed as a very audacious fellow, indeed. He had nerve; everyone said so. In the excitement of having seen Peg hit in the nose, the boys almost forgot about Richard, who stood about, wondering, holding his head and complaining again and again that Mark had torn his sweater on purpose.

But Mark was reasonably happy; he was ready for any respect that might be forthcoming. Miss Matthews blamed him for starting the fight with Peg; he could have denied it, but having the blame would heighten his reputation. To start a fight with Peg!—that was unprecedented! He had walked right up and socked Peg in the nose. No one had ever done that before.

And even though his head still rang, his stomach no longer had that sick feeling. In the boy's lavatory, where he held his head under the faucet to stop his nose bleed, he was casually handed a paper towel by Ossie Ferguson, who was a close friend of Ted Brown and himself a fifth-grader. "Gee," Mark said, "thank you."

"You kind of got some blood on you," Ossie told him. Mark made a useless gesture to wipe it off; it was his good blue sweater, but with his head down, he murmured, "It's just bloody," as though his sweaters were always like that.

But his sweater was bright with it. What would his mother say? He looked at Ossie, as though to draw reassurance from him, but Ossie kicked the door open with his foot and walked out. "Can't no one come in," Mark heard him say importantly to the fellows outside, for Miss Matthews had told him to keep the boys away from Mark.

For most of that afternoon Mark had to sit alone in the principal's office; that was part of his punishment. Mr. Blake was away, but Mark could not return to class until he talked to Mr. Blake and asked to be forgiven. What other punishment he would receive would be decided upon later, the teacher said, in an awesome tone. Mark did not mind. Miss. Matthews had patted his head before she left, and even in the dark of the room his bruises felt warm and amiable.

He found that if he closed his eyes, he saw scenes from his fight with Richard, and these sickened him; he would jump to his feet and talk out loud, and then he would feel bad all over. But if he thought of Peg, he felt all right. Now that no one could see him, he swung his tired right arm back and forth, hitting and smashing nose, over and over again, until the poor thing became a mangled pulp; and as he swung his arm, he could once more see that astonished face as his fist hit it. And even his fist felt good.

There was the chance that Peg might seek revenge for his humiliation, but Mark doubted it, for nobody would like Peg if he did. Anyway, Peg had to stay after school tonight and Mark had to stay the next night. By then Peg would be thinking of other things.

Thirteenth Chapter

THE ANTE-ROOM was a good place to be. After an hour the darkness in there became as kind to Mark as a blanket; he knew that just outside the shutters was daylight, for through the cracks came fingers of it, to reach here and there and touch his knees. The room itself felt warm and snug, so that it became a world of its own, made up of two benches, a desk and a table, separated by good walls from the world outside, but quite beyond the people there.

Mark healed in this place, which had become his own; indeed, he was so much better in a while that he must have almost fallen asleep, because, before he knew it, Miss Matthews was in the room and had turned on the lights. He stared at her, blinking; she wasn't like the Statue at all. Would she slap his hands? Or would she be like she used to be, when she came to his house?

She had a paper bag and put his blue sweater in it. Miss Matthews said she was disappointed in him;

she was also ashamed of him. Mark felt his eyes tighten, but he determined that he would not cry in front of his teacher. He would have to stay after school a long time tomorrow night, she said, but he could go home now if he wanted to. But he did not want to go. Home—that was where he would have to tell his mother. Miss Matthews told him to wash his face again, then, and come back to class.

When his face was wet with cold water, Mark was glad that he was going back to class, for he had to return there sometime, and it would be all right now, for the fellows would remember that he had hit Peg right in the nose. For the moment Richard was forgotten.

However, there was still Judith. She was part of the dreadful hush that greeted him when he entered the room. She was watching him closely and fearfully; and, without even looking at her, Mark knew it. She would be sitting miserably at her desk and thinking that horrible things had happened to him.

If his knee and spirit could have had their way, Mark would have been able to limp into the room, thus to get a certain glory from his wound; but he knew he had to contend with Judith's feelings. If he limped, she was likely to cry. She had been known to do that. Judith would cry in school, even, if she felt like it; and anything else she pleased, for look how she had kissed him. And when she began crying, you just couldn't stop her, for she refused to listen, like that time she had seen a baseball hit him in the head. She kept crying even when he showed her his head, so that she could see for herself that it did not have a crack in it.

Therefore, Mark not only had to forego the pleasure of limping a little, but he had to pretend to be happy all afternoon. But you could not fool Judith. When school was over finally, she got out of the room first and was waiting for him at the door, but he avoided her by walking out with a bunch of boys, who made a great deal of noise talking. Judith hesitated, and then she was too late, for he was gone. He glanced back furtively and saw her still by the door; Richard came from the room and walked past her, but she did not speak to him.

Mark hurried on; as soon as he was out of her sight, he ducked down Blair Street and cut home the back way, from the other side of town. It was longer that way, but it was worth it, for he was sure that he wished to speak to no one. Any other time he would have enjoyed speaking of his fight to some of the fellows he respected, but now he had his report to his mother to think about. What should he say? It was all Judith's fault; there was no doubt about that. Richard had done wrong, too. He was through with that fellow; he would never go to his house again. He could keep his old house. Still, he could not tell his mother all that; but he must explain his knee. Well, he had been fighting. Lots of people did that, especially in the third and fourth grades. And he was getting older now. That ought to be explanation enough . . . Mark decided that he wanted to tell his mother right away. He hurried, for then he would would be done with the whole thing.

Even so, Judith must have reached his house before he did. She must have run straight from school, for someone had rang the door bell; but when his mother answered it, no one was there. A note, though, was pinned on the door, and upon the note was what seemed to be a valentine, hastily drawn in the shape of a broken heart.

The day, however, was not St. Valentine's and the heart with the great crack in it was but a preamble and a symbol for the alarming message on the inside of the folded paper.

"Peg Sooley," it said, "is after Mark. Mark hit Peg. Blame is not Mark but me."

Just that, the note said; but it meant more than that to Mark's mother. It had no salutation and no signature, but Judith wrote it, of course; he realized that immediately. No one but Judith could spell such hard words, and certainly no other person in the town had such a lack of shame as to pin a note with a broken heart upon his mother's front door.

His mother said that this was terrible—not the note, but the way Mark was acting lately. He was becoming a creature of the wild. She didn't know what she was going to do with him.

His knee was her first consideration. He had to hold it up for a long time while she looked at it. Then he had to take off all his clothes and have a bath. There was a drop of blood on the front of his shirt and when she saw it, she caught her breath. And then, of course, he had to tell her all about the fight.

"But I'm not badly hurt," he said, in conclusion, to make her feel better.

Indeed, he wished he could tell her how he had turned defeat into victory, but when he saw how she felt, he had no words for it. There were getting to be things that he could not say because she disliked him to say them. Telling her even this much made him very uncomfortable. He was relieved, and quite happy, when it was over and his knee was bandaged; and he had promised never, never to fight again.

"But what if they hit me first?" he wanted to know.

"Then you must run and tell Miss Matthews."

"But, Mom, they'll call me a sissy, like Rodney Fowler!"

She knew a way in which even that crisis could be ended. "If that happens, don't you care what they call you. Remember—'Sticks and stones may break my bones, but words will never hurt me'." And she gave his shoulder a reassuring pat.

She said she would write a letter to Miss Matthews tomorrow, and he would have to bring it to school, for the note would apologize for his conduct.

But that would spoil everything. Mark was suddenly apprehensive. He tried to tell her how such a note would bring to an immediate end the respect he had gained with such difficulty. "I'll never fight anyone again, ever, if you don't write that to her!" And his tone was so beseeching that she hesitated. "Think of what the fellows would say!" he pointed out. "Just don't write that note, Mother." He was pleading as hard as he could.

His mother looked down at him. "We shall see," she said, in that wise and distant tone that mothers sometimes use.

But she would not write it; Mark could see that. He sighed, and limped upstairs to bed.

The fight was over, but the fuss was not. From his bedroom, where he lay in bed in the bright daylight, like a martyr compelled to see the world but forbidden to live in it, he could hear from way downstairs the faint sound of his mother speaking over the telephone. Once he thought he heard her laugh, and many times he heard her say "Isobel." She was talking to his enemy's mother; maybe they would be angry, too; but it was then that he thought he heard her laugh. When she came upstairs, he asked her if she had laughed, but she said emphatically that she had not. "The idea," she said, "children in school fighting like ruffians in the street!"

That evening she let him come downstairs for supper, although he was not very hungry. He was having his dessert when Miss Matthews came to visit. He thought that perhaps he should not be in his nightgown, but she failed to notice it. He watched her kiss his mother; he was afraid she was going to kiss him, but she only pinched his cheek and said, "Somebody likes sweets."

"He's a cake-eater," his mother said, and Miss Matthews pinched his cheek again.

And right after that, his mother made him go back to bed. He did not mind it so much, for his house was different with Miss Matthews here; he knew they were going to talk about him. Still, he was glad to go.

Mark did not stay in bed, though, for he heard Miss Matthews' voice rising higher, and then he heard them both laugh; and he crept from bed and slipped to the stairway, and there, pressed against the railing, he looked down at them. His feet were cold and he could not lean on his sore knee, but he had to see what they were doing. From up here, Miss Matthews looked smaller; in fact, every time he saw her, she seemed to change a little. She was smiling and talking now in a way she never did at school. With a gasp, he saw that his mother had done the worst thing possible; she had showed Judith's note to Miss Matthews, so that she laughed in little shrieks. "Father and daughter are of the same mind," he heard her say, "for I'll tell you in confidence," and then she began a story that Mark could but partly hear. He heard her mention Mr. Blake and the janitor; she said she had never seen him "take on so" as he did with that janitor. She kept repeating that it would have done his mother's heart good to see the way he enquired about Mark.

"And that's not all," he heard her say, "but he's as interested in Mark's work, I think, as he is in his own child's.

"I tell you," she said, "that you just should have seen how he took on when he returned. You'd have thought we'd all been to blame."

Mark heard his mother answer her, but she spoke so low he could not hear what she said.

"Well," he heard Miss Matthews say, "I wouldn't think another thing of it. I'm going to keep him and the Souley boy after school tomorrow night, and before we're through we'll all be the best of friends."

His mother asked Miss Matthews what she thought of the new wave of influenza in the east, so Mark, not at all ashamed for having listened, crept back to bed. His feet were cold and he was a long time getting them warm again. "I'll never be friends with him," he said, almost out loud, "never, because he'll never be friends with me." He vowed that when he became a second-grader he would do something awful to Peg. Just what, he did not know; but it would be awful, all right. Furthermore, he would hate him all his life; and tomorrow, on his way to school, he would carry a rock.

How long Mark had this hate, or if the next day he did choose a rock, there is no way of knowing.

The evening was easily remembered because of its objects and incidents; his bruised knee, the unexpected visitor, the hall, the stairway, Miss Matthews' and his mother's voices—when he recalled one, he invariably included the others, for the association of one led swiftly to another. But he could recall nothing beyond that evening to indicate the outcome of its promise. Memory is uneasy and restless, and when time lowers upon it and gathers weight, an incident is pressed into a succession of things; and sometimes when you try to grasp that incident, it is gone.

A month had passed—a month, a year, a day; time turned wrong beyond all reason, so that in his mind when memory at last found a high place, Mark had moved into a world far wider, and yet not as round and clear as the one he had left. There was a dark and warm kind of sickness, the soldiers came, and people died; and those who lived were different persons than they had been before. Mark had the influenza.

Fourteenth Chapter

THAT WAS the year something happened to the sun. The boy, so quick to personification, knew it had stayed high in the heavens, aloof and impartial, until the deep winter season, but then the earth turned from it, and the sun no longer showed its face.

Every day was cloudy, and night came more swiftly than ever it came before; there was no rain, yet the air was wet and thick, and the ground never dried from one day to the next. The days themselves hung heavily, for the wind was gone, leaving the trees listless; and in the town, above the buildings, the many proud flags, like the days, hung down in defeat. Each morning the sun was expected, and each morning people in that part of the west looked to the sky with wavering trust.

As long as people could remember they had never seen the like before, but wonder turned from amazement to a kind of fear, and that brought superstition. When science was unable to find a satisfactory reason, an explanation, at least, that Colburn could understand, then the oldest men in the town were consulted; nothing but foreboding came forth from them. Each day the newspapers were searched for this suitable reason, but the news was that influenza was spreading. France and the trenches were replaced by reports from American cities, where this sickness alone had become the concern. Until now the influenza had been under control, but something had happened, for this time more people were dying than had been sick before. It was worse in the west, for the sun was gone—gone even from such an important place as San Francisco. In the cities, cases appeared once again and doctors found in them a new kind of fever.

The people of Colburn began to wait at the depot to meet the train that came in the afternoon, for it carried the newspapers from the cities, but even the newspapers could not say exactly what influenza was, except that it was something that came in wartime. It came from France, from China; it was a scourge in the steerage of ships. Rats were its carriers. It was in the air. But some people were confident that influenza came from Mexico and was brought across the border by members of the I.W.W.; and learned men guessed that it grew in the bodies of soldiers in training camps; but other people in Colburn had found out it was something scientific that the German Imperial Army had negotiated to spread on the food of American citizens.

But through it all, there were still a few families in Colburn who believed that the evils of influenza had been exaggerated, for there were ways to keep it away, and nearly everyone complied by again wearing a gauze mask and boiling one's handkerchiefs; but no one knew why the sun was gone.

Before long, though, the simple precautions were no longer precaution enough. The nearest city, which was also without sunshine, reported case after case; in time, in a very short time, in a week—there was an epidemic. Where one case had been, there were two; then ten, and a dozen, a score; and, finally, where there had been one case, now there was a hundred. Then people realized that influenza was really a plague.

Still, the plague was in the cities, in the large and indefinite places of the east; everyone said that it would surely not come to such a small town as Colburn. They tried to have comfort in that. The town would be all right when the sun came through again.

The sickness, though, wished for more than cities, for the time came when two cases, both together, were reported in Mark's town. They came so suddenly that even though the doctors were prepared, no one knew exactly what should be done. Isolation, of course; but what treatment? Keep the patients resting, boil the water, and watch their pulse.

The first two victims were a man and his wife. They were two of the town's most admirable citizens. Childless, they were both in middle life and prosperous, so that they could travel more than most people. They became ill the Tuesday after a week-end in the city; at noontime the husband had to come home from his office. His head was light, and, when he walked, his legs moved forward almost of their own accord. His wife fell into a fever that night. And on the second night, the nurse said, he awakened from a restless dream and demanded to see his wife, but she was dead; and he himself slipped down into a sleep and this time did not awaken. When word came of their death, people pretended astonishment and said that it was not possible, for just last week they had served staunchly on the Red Cross committee.

Only the church came forward with an explanation. These were times of great duress, but the work of the business man and his wife on the earth was done and God had called them to Heaven. But the doctors were concerned with more material matters; they consulted together, the three of them, and decided the bodies must not be laid to view in funeral. That caused great wonder, but the doctors were adamant. People said that a horrible thing had happened. The bodies had turned black in a night.

But there was little time left to wonder. The dead had scarcely been buried; indeed, news of the sickness had scarcely reached the ears of the ranchers, before the town's oldest doctor, almost seventy, complained of a ringing in his head and a fever. His sons sent for his colleagues, but the aged one insisted it could not be influenza that he had. Why, influenza attacked those in adolescence and middle life. The very young and the very old were immune, almost. His word bore weight; he was a very great doctor and he had personally considered his symptoms. His associates were inclined to agree with him; he could not have influenza.

But it was that; and in two days, the old doctor, like Adam, like Seth, and Noah, was dead.

Then cases were reported so rapidly that influenza became an incubus and people lost count of their sick. The swiftness and fecundity, the mystery of it; they were so terrifying. It was a stranger, inevitable and ruthless, immune to all of the standard home-treatments and scornful of the oldest herb cures of the oldest grandmothers.

How could the government allow this plague from another world; and how could God stand for it, the people wanted to know. Was it the War? Was it part of this weather? Or was the War the cause of it all? What was it that came into a body and caused it to die in a day? Some people said there was bound to be a plague because the sun was gone, and other people suggested that the sun was gone because of cannonading in France, for explosions caused clouds to gather and rain to fall. But that was in France. People here were peaceful.

If only the sun would shine again the dream would end and the incubus with it. Yet thirty days had passed, one slowly after the other, without the sun appearing, as the heavens knew it should; and still there were people who prayed and looked to the sky with a certain trust.

For Mark, though, these matters were scarcely of first concern. He had been a very sick boy, as everybody said, but there was so much excitement that when he started to get well, he was seldom noticed; but there was one good thing, his mother said, of his having been sick before the plague really began. He was able to have a doctor.

When Mark finally got to his feet, he found he preferred to sit down; and then, before he knew it, he had taken a nap. It seemed to him that he slept for days at a time. And when at last he could go out in the yard, he wobbled about like the first colt of spring. The day was cloudy and the air was warm and thick, yet when he stood in the yard, he saw a world more beautiful than any he could remember. It was so large.

It did not seem strange to him that the weather should be warm in the middle of winter, and he was puzzled only occasionally that he could not see the sun. There were things in his life more puzzling than that. He was sorry for everyone, but he had barely come into his memory; if the sun broke a precedent of a hundred years, he must not be expected to realize it.

Perhaps Mark had not lived long enough to learn to rely upon the sun. He had accepted it, while it was up there, and more than once it had caught his attention, so that he stared in surprise. He missed it now that it was gone; he was not startled, though, at anything the sun might do.

His mother said there would be no more school for a long time and that he must continue to do exactly as she bid him. He stayed in his yard, he wore his mask; he kept his hands away from his mouth, whenever he happened to remember that they were straying in that direction; and he talked to no one who walked by his house.

Mark was on an island, but in the town people still became sick and died. Influenza went through a family in a week, killing some of the children and leaving others weak and sleepy. There was talk at this time of burning all homes where influenza had succeeded; and one night two houses did catch fire. But hoodlums had fired the houses, and the next day they did not receive the praise they had expected.

The streets in daytime were deserted; the doctors hurried from one house to another, and a man who volunteered to crank and drive a car for the doctors, was spoken of as a hero. Five nurses arrived by railroad; and the newspaper said the government would come to the aid of Colburn. Mark awakened one day to great excitement, for a strange doctor was going to live in his house; later, he was disappointed, for the doctor used only his father's office. Mark was forbidden to go in and look at him, but he often saw him as he entered and left by the side door.

The district where the dredgermen lived was the hardest hit of all. Influenza swept from one family to another, like a fire that could not be seen. The dredgers lay idle giants in the earth and many of the men left town, but most of them could not, for they had children at home with fever.

Mark's mother and other ladies sent jellies and blankets and broths to the district, and even in the city prayers were offered for the dredger people; but the district was doomed. The soldiers came and isolated it; no one but doctors and nurses could enter or leave.

There was not time enough to bury the bodies in caskets. Immediate burial was necessary; some were burned, but most bodies were wrapped in blankets and put in the earth, in a field beyond the church, where grave diggers sometimes held lanterns at night.

Although it was worse in the dredgermen's district, the entire town was stricken. Trading stopped. The grocer left his bundles at the gates of the houses. People were afraid to go to the postoffice for their mail. The doctor who stayed at Mark's house, no longer bothered to remove his clothes when he came back to the office to sleep; he fell into his cot. Mark knew, for one morning he saw his mother shake him.

Fifteenth Chapter

YET THE fatigue, the disease, and fear in the town gave Mark little anxiety. He was not afraid, and he was seldom sorry that people were dying; in truth, he was never so sad nor frightened but that he was first, and most of all, curious. He did not want to see a dead one, but his feeling was the same as if he wished to go close, to know without looking.

When his mother received the telephone call that Miss Matthews had died, and impulsively came to him weeping, he wept only because the moment inspired it. Then he closed his mind on his dead teacher, appearing to forget her so fast she may never have lived; yet for days after that, in which he was happy, he avoided the telephone, as though he played some kind of game in which the rule was that he must keep a wide circle around it.

Watching him and estimating the depth of his feeling from his reactions, nearly anyone in that town, except perhaps his mother, would believe him scarcely human. His teacher was dead; and if he cared, he hardly showed it, at least not in words or action that an adult could comprehend.

And though Mark and his mother seemed to communicate with an emotion rather than thought, there were times when even she must not always have been able to follow him, because sometimes she asked, when he was remote from her, why he had suddenly become so distant or what he was thinking about in such a solemn fashion. If she insisted, he became strangely confused and stammered that he did not know, which was the truth, in a measure, for it was as though he had been to a place that she could not come. An obscure and secret place to her, perhaps, was this place where his thoughts were moving, but surely familiar to him. Yet he had no words to tell her where or what they were, nor could he take her to them.

The thoughts of a child, like water slipping past in a brook, run without bidding, translucent to light and elusive in their reverie. The adult who looks there, looks through water; could he touch the stream, he would know it chilling.

That may be the reason Mark indicated neither grief nor fear when he heard that Judith had influenza. She became ill one evening; she said her body hurt all over and that her head felt funny. At eight o'clock that night Judith's mother, a coat thrown around her shoulders, came to Mark's house for the doctor. Mark had to remain upstairs, but he heard Mrs. Blake describe the symptoms and his mother ask if Judith had a fever, and he saw Mrs. Blake look at her with her face wrinkled up, so that he knew she was crying. Mark lay at the top of the staircase, where he had often waited with his wooden rifle to intercept Indians that sped through the valley of the hall rug below.

His mother was telephoning, trying to locate the doctor, while Judith's mother walked up and down before her and sometimes turned to the telephone, as though to grab it away. Even while his mother was 'phoning, Mrs. Blake kept repeating that her husband was frantic.

Mark saw his mother drop the telephone and start toward his father's office; he wondered what she was going to do. But she hesitated, turned, and ran up the stairs. She found him pressed against the staircase and kneeled beside him; she was telling him that she would be right back and that there was nothing for him to be afraid of, and that he should not worry, for Judith would be all right. She hugged him, then left him to dart into her bedroom for her coat. She called to him that he must go to bed right away and that she would return as soon as he fell asleep. "Promise?" she said, and he promised, for he was already in his nightgown.

Downstairs, Mrs. Blake was sitting by the telephone, leaning over with her face in her hands. His mother touched her and whispered something, but Mrs. Blake did not reply. He saw his mother run into his father's office, and the light flashed on. She took something from the cabinet and ran back to Mrs. Blake. Then, as he watched, she was gone; the door closed, but he lay against the staircase for a moment, trembling with excitement.

It was the first time that he could remember that he was left in the house alone at night. Then he was brave; he would be a brave man. People would say how brave he was; why, he could be a soldier.

For a moment Mark must have forgotten that his mother was gone, for he jumped to his feet to run to ask her if he could be a soldier. And when he remembered, a chill moved up his neck and touched his hair like a light hand. He shook it away, but a feeling of fear came over him that he had never felt before. It was not that he had been left alone, or that the dark things in the house looked strange, although the shadow from that big chair did become an awful thing. This fear was because of something within him, as if one part of himself was afraid of another. He knew he was not a bit afraid personally, but his body was; his head kept turning around so that his eyes could look in all directions. He told himself not to do that, but he did it just the same.

"Stop!" he gruffly told himself, and with the house so quiet, his voice sounded very loud. "Don't be afraid," he said, "nothing's going to hurt you," but this time he whispered. Somebody might hear him. Mark leaned against the stairway and listened very quietly.

At first, he could hardly hear a thing; but in a moment, as though it came from far away, he heard the clock in the parlor. He never knew that he could hear it way upstairs, but he could hear it quite distinctly now. He and the clock were alone in the house. Tick tock, hickory dock; he could not help but listen to it. His thoughts slowed down to the beat of the clock.

Te-ick te-ock, hick-ory dock; I like to breathe, says the clock, te-ick te-ock. It was getting louder. Suddenly, Mark was horrified. The clock was coming *closer!* It was *walking,* te-ick te-ock, slowly along, te-ick te-ock. The clock-was-in the-dining-room, te-ick te-ock, the grandfather's clock, old-and-funny, brown-in-a-box, te-ick te-ock, like breathing—no, like *walking up the stairs!*

Mark stayed there no longer. He fled to the bathroom, terrified, groped for the door and slammed it as hard as he could, and pressed himself against it. In a moment he was safe enough to use one of his hands to wipe his eyes; his nose was full, too, but he did not care; why, the old clock couldn't get him, what was there to cry about, anyway? It was just a clock.

Mark faintly remembered a story about a clock and Mr. Anderson's wife. He had never seen her; therefore, she must have died a long time ago; but he had heard about her. Perhaps he had overheard his mother discussing her, or someone had told him; anyway, the clock had done something to her and she had died. His father had told her not to raise her hands over her head, not even to wind the clock. But she had, and her heart had hurt. That was a long time ago. Yet he remembered there was a story about it, for he had wondered how she could have been sick from a clock.

Now Judith was sick. Perhaps he would be sick again; that would be awful. How bad it would be, he could tell by the lump that came up his throat when he thought about it; but he really wasn't ill, he knew. Standing on the wooden box that his father had painted for him, Mark washed his teeth, and then he looked into the mirror a long time at his face.

For the first time now, in a great while, he remembered how his father looked. He had not tried to remember; the image just came to his mind. Mostly, when he thought of him, he saw a father that towered over him in dark clothes, someone who picked him up and laughed at him. But now he saw his father quite clearly, his face, the large, straight nose, and his glasses with the light twisting in them; Mark even remembered his white collars, odd and stiff, they were, and smooth to touch.

The picture, though, that Mark most often had of his father came when people asked him if his father had got a Hun for him yet, so that he had come to imagine him in a soldier suit in France, a vast place not unlike the pine forest beyond Mark's house, where in the daytime his father searched for Huns. He decided, however, that by now he must be on his way home, for Mark could see him already; and somehow, he was in Mark's bedroom, taking off his coat. If his father were here tonight, he would go in and sleep with him.

It seemed to him that his mother had been gone a long time; it must be very late at night. If she came home and found him awake, there would be trouble. But if he left the bathroom, he would have to turn out the light. His mother had lighted the light above his bed, and if only he could leave the bathroom light burning, he could walk clear to his room without touching the dark.

Tonight, though, he was not afraid of the dark; not really. It was just that he did not wish to turn out the bathroom light until he had gone to bed, and even then it would be nice to have it on. There was something bright and clean and bare about the bathroom, when the light was on; it was like standing in the sunlight, except that the dark was nearer than it was in the daytime.

So Mark left the bathroom, with the light still shining behind him, and but partly closed the door. He gave the corridor a searching look, much like his father may have given the pine forests of France, and then walked noisily to his room.

His father kept some of his things in Mark's bedroom, a row of brown and glum-looking books, the boots he wore in the woods; and in a corner of the closet was his father's dismantled fishing pole. But Mark was forbidden to touch that. On the top shelf, and long neglected, was the old satchel that his father had carried before Mark and his mother put their money together to give him a new case for his birthday present.

Mark was standing in the doorway of the closet, considering whether his mother would let him have that old satchel, when suddenly he felt very sorry for himself. He must have been almost an adult at that moment, for he felt that he was cheated of his father, as people said, and that Richard had picked on him that day in the kitchen, and that if only his father were here, he would not be left alone like this. And it was almost with desperation, through eyes that were blinking, that he stared into the closet. The corduroy suit was there, way in the back, behind his own things; and it looked so large, and somehow seemed like his father, that Mark sobbed in relief and ran to it. But he did not cry; he clung to the suit until he felt better.

Mark did not go to bed until he was shivering. His room was cold, even though it was heavy and thick with the close dead air of the town. His head felt stuffy and he was very tired. He climbed into bed before he took off his bathrobe. Leaning down, he placed his slippers, side by side, by the bed, taking care to get them exactly even; and then he lay back in his bathrobe until the sheets were warmer.

He got up on his knees, after a moment, and skinned out of his robe, looked all around the room, and then turned out the light, to slip far under the blankets as fast as he could. He did not put his head underneath the covers, though; he did that only when the bed was a submarine about to go under the sea. Instead, he kept his head barely above, for he wished to see the shaft of light that came shining to him through the darkness of the hall. Then, before he knew it, he was asleep.

Mark awakened very early that morning. Men were cutting wood in the forest nearby, but he knew it was early because the rest of the world was so quiet. He listened a moment longer, still very drowsy, until in a quick excitement he remembered last night. He jumped from bed, forgetting his slippers so carefully placed, and ran into his mother's room.

But she was still asleep; and, without really awakening, she moved over slowly to make room for him. The sheets were just cold enough to exhilarate him. He wanted his mother to speak to him so that he could begin telling her all the things that he knew; but he did not know if he should speak first. She was awakening, though. She looked at him slowly and drew her hair back from her forehead; and then she realized he was there. He shouted with delight, but she put her arm around him and drew him down to the pillow, and murmured something. He asked her what she said, and she shook her head and smiled.

"Don't you worry," she told him, "she'll be all right." Mark looked puzzled. "Judith," she said, and he remembered.

And after a moment, she added, "She's very sick, but she will be all right, by and by."

There were some questions that Mark intended to ask, but he had forgotten what they were; he wanted to learn more of last night, but it was morning now, and last night was so far away that it seemed of no importance.

His mother was wide awake now and smiling at him ruefully. "There'll be no sun today," she said. "The air's so thick you can twist it."

"Ho," he laughed at her, "you can't twist air!" But the sun reminded him of last night and what he had to tell his mother, for he knew that he had been but partly true to his trust. "Mother," he said, unsteadily, "I'm sorry I left the bathroom light on."

Sixteenth Chapter

MARK DID not consider that his mother could be mistaken. Her words could usually guide him from his troubles; they gave him the comfort they had failed to give Judith's mother. Perhaps that was the reason, or it may have been that he was concerned only with himself, that he had no concern for Judith after that morning in bed.

A few mornings later, though, when he complained that because he had to stay home all the time he had nothing to do, his mother told him that he should think of something nice to do for Judith; perhaps in his play things he could find her a present, to bring to her when she was well again. "That will give you something to think about," she said, "and now, right now, I'll give you something to do." And she sent him to the basement to gather some kindling for the breakfast fire.

But down in the basement Mark became so preoccupied with what he would do for Judith, that he sat down on a stick of wood and forgot about the kindling. His mother called to him to hurry, but before he reached the kitchen range with the kindling, he had been given a scolding. She told him to go out in the yard, to be out of her way until breakfast time. He was glad to go; he was wearing his overalls, which meant that he could climb around as much as he pleased.

The ground in the yard was damp. He tried skidding, but he was not very successful. As far as he could see in the sky, in every direction, the sun was not in sight; and school would not begin until the sun shined. People said that if it would only rain, the sun would come out, and then everybody would be well.

Judith's house across the way was quiet. Nearby a bobolink sang, two hasty notes, clear but out of tune in this morning. Mark climbed the fence, to get a better look at Judith's place. There was no smoke from the chimney; it was just a gray house; bare, except for the rose bushes, now rusted with winter. But way in the back of the house an electric lamp was still burning, a faded yellow in the morning light.

"No one is up," Mark said to himself, "and they've left the light on for Judith."

He noticed the branches of the rose bushes. They looked so thin and sharp he thought they might even be as sharp as *spies*. Mark knew a great deal about spies. The enemy wore them and people talked about them. The Huns, the I.W.W.s, Mexicans, and the Germans had them, but sometimes they did not wear their spies. They hid them, and people said Look Out for Spies! and for a good reason, for they were very sharp. Only the fiercest soldiers wore spies all the time, and they wore them on their shiny helmets, and those were the unfairest weapons of all, for when an American soldier was wounded, the Huns and I.W.W.s jumped upon him as he fell, to stick him in the stomach with their spies. The Indians, though, were just as bad; they carried tomahawks.

It was a different kind of war that the Indians had; for one thing, there were no gas masks. He guessed that his gauze mask could pretend to be a gas mask. Mark ran into the house to get it, and when he returned, he was in a gas attack, watching through a crack in the fence for soldiers wearing spies . . . But a moment later, the yard rang with a trumpet call; and all around him, from all sides, came his brave comrades, the Texas Rangers. He and his men were well armed with long rifles and bowie knives, and along the rail of the high board fence they clanked on their careful vigil, guarding the road a few yards away against an attack of desperate Mexicans.

But his men fled from him in a twinkling when Mark saw that there was someone who could see him. A man driving a horse and cart was coming slowly along the road. Mark watched him suspiciously. What was this man doing, driving along the road? The man saw him and waved; and as he came alongside the fence, he spoke to Mark and slackened the reins to let his horse rest a moment. Mark did not know him, but the man knew his name.

"What're you doing up so early, Mark? Looking for trouble?"

Mark shook his head. He noticed the horse was more brown than he was black; maybe the man would let him ride in the cart some day.

"Have you heard from your daddy?" the man asked.

"He's going to get the Kaiser," Mark told the man, for someone had once told him so. The words did not mean exactly what they said, but people liked him to say them.

"Sure he is!" the man replied. "He ought to be home with him any day now."

He waved a finger across his mouth. "I'll tell you a secret," he said, "but you can't tell anyone I told you." Mark nodded. "Well," the man said, "just this morning I nearly got a Hun for myself!"

Where! Mark wanted to know.

The man chuckled. "Never mind where . . . But do you know what's under the sack in my buckboard? Well, that's a bomb!"

Mark drew back in alarm; he had to wave his arms to retain his balance on the fence rail.

"What kind of a bomb?" he said, taking another breath.

"I found it on my farm," the man told him. "The Huns put it there last night to blow me up . . . But I guess I get up too early for 'em."

Mark wanted to know what he intended to do with it. Was it right there, under the sack—really?

"Want to see it?" the man asked him.

"I guess I have to go in and eat breakfast," Mark replied.

"All right," said the man, "but you'd better keep your eye on this fence . . . I mean, this whole road around your house. And if you find any bombs around, you'll get a medal.

"You can't tell," he added, "there might be some Huns right around here now . . . Ain't that right?"

But Mark knew now that this was just some of that heavy nonsense adults used when they wanted to play with children. "Aw," he said, to indicate he was hard to fool.

"Don't be too sure," he was warned. "You can't always tell."

"Now I have to go eat breakfast," Mark told him.

The man chuckled. "Don't forget," he said, "I'm depending on you to watch this road." He picked up the reins and urged the horse forward. "Don't get too many Germans," he called back.

Mark slid down the fence and started toward his house. He felt a breeze against his face; and then, although he could hardly believe it, he felt a few

- 241 -

drops of rain. He ran full speed to the kitchen. "Mom!" he called, "it's raining!" But when she looked out of the window, she shook her head. "It's looked this way for days," she said.

Mark went in to wash his hands, and when he returned, he slid across the linoleum to the table. He pulled up a chair and sat down with a thump. It was a good place to be; a gentle heat came from the range, and there was a magazine there with brightly colored pictures. The pages were so smooth that he liked to touch them.

If Mark heard the footsteps on the backporch, he must have thought someone from town was picking up the laundry. He heard his mother talking, though; but even as he looked up, she closed the back door. She was gone a long time, and he had looked at almost all of the pictures; he did not hear his mother return at all, until he felt her arms around him.

"Mark," she said, and paused. "Mark, do you remember what Daddy says when people become so tired and sick that they don't want their bodies anymore? They go to live in Heaven."

He wondered what she meant. "Mark," she said, "Judith's gone to live in Heaven."

She was crying, and to see her crying, in the room so quiet, made him cry, too. He sobbed and put his head against her almost as if he was angry. "You said she wouldn't!" he told her. "You said she wouldn't do it!"

For the second time his mother was mistaken, for that was the morning it rained. Mark saw the first drops as they fell on the windowpane, and he watched as they made brown marks in the dust on the sill . . . Seeing him there, his mother may have thought he was thinking of Judith, but he was wondering what happened to the rain when it hit the wood.

It was the first rain in two months, and this was the winter season. But the sun did not follow, as his mother expected, for the rain stopped before noon and the sky remained gray and dull.

Mark cried only once more that day, and this time it was with less emotion than the rain. He had eaten lunch and drunk two glasses of milk, and then he wanted to go out and play, but his mother would not let him go. She was at the sink, doing the dishes, and when he looked at her, he saw there were tears in her eyes.

Then he cried, and went back to the table and sat down. He wondered where Judith was now, but that was too mysterious. A moment later he became interested in the linoleum squares on the floor; he gave a hop-scotch hop, and then another. He gave a great leap, and called to his mother to show her he had jumped three squares.

Seventeenth Chapter

IN TIME the influenza ended. Precisely when, Mark
was never able to tell, for as soon as it ended it was
a long time ago; and so many things had happened
at once. One day the sun was shining, he could remove his mask to go out and play once more, and
even the war itself was over.

In memory it seemed to him a day; in the world's
time it may have been a week, more likely longer;
but for him these three astonishing events became a
dazzling triune, built like an arch to his excitement.
The influenza and its effects, the weeks of it, became
the things that happened in the night before that
day. A night and a day, in a child's mind, then;
oppression and sickness, relief and triumph, run
through with an undertone of eerie emotion—they
were separated only by one sun.

Judith's death, but not Judith, was soon gone from
his mind. He seldom referred to her, and remembered her only because he did not wish to speak of

her, for to do that would be an awful thing. When his mother mentioned Judith, he felt embarrassed, as though a discourtesy had been committed.

And in these memories of the day and the night, recent though they were, Judith was not included. Even though she had taken sick and died during the period his imagination concentrated into a night (and somehow, it was the night he was left alone), she remained, nevertheless, entirely apart from it, so that he recalled her much less than he did that period, which returned to him many times, in forms that he could not understand.

Mark had slept through that night, and it was as if he had slept through the sickness of that period; somehow they were the same, one long night that he learned of gradually. Parts of it came to him, shreds of conversation, odds and ends of people's actions—these he put together, piece by piece, unknowingly in search of a pattern that stayed mysterious and beyond him, until in time he felt that upon that night there had been a hideous enchantment, vast and green, like the one in which the Knight was bewitched until Beauty broke the spell.

Lack of sunlight in that time had caused the deep green plants to flourish; mosses and ivy sought to obscure windows and doors, and the damp crept into the houses to settle beneath carpets and under the leather in chairs. In the thickness of the air, it lay like beads of fever upon ledges and tables; even the wood in the walls seemed wet, or so Mark believed, as he remembered the time, for all the morbid things of that year, those fogs and impenetrable mysteries of living that a child knows, settled into that night, like dampness to a low place.

When, in the deep grass, he upturned a rock and saw what was underneath; when during a rainy morning the dining room gave back the dead smell of food eaten there on Sundays long before; when he noticed that fruit, though carefully arranged in bowls, in time turned saccharine and soft, to infect one another; when in an old house he smelled a musty hallway, or saw the dog behind the butcher shop turn and snap in his sleep; whenever, indeed, he remembered the man who wanted bulrushes, or saw a light in a house burning yellow, and heard the cry of a sick child—then these and others, by some odd association in his mind, became part of that night; and that night itself was a thick green growth that covered a certain time of night.

Abruptly for him it ended with the end of the war, and that came late one night, just before dawn, when Mark was awakened by the noise of crowds. Voices were meeting together and coming in triumph to his house. Even as he listened, bells began to ring, first one and then another, so that he awakened excited, thrilled by so much noise where there should be silence. He shivered as he did in only the darkest hours, before the most special occasions . . .

Above the bells now, he heard a whistle shriek

from the factory, again a great clanging of bells; then, after a pause, another loud cry reached him, as though it had hesitated for the strength of many voices, and brought them together, like a wave gathers water, to his house. Mark sprang to the floor and ran headlong into his mother's room, gasping "Fire! Fire!" as excited and puzzled as could be.

But his mother knew what had happened. She slipped out of her bed and ran to the window, where by the light of the sky she tried to look down to the town. She brushed her hair back from her face and looked again. And in another moment she had laughed and hugged him, leaving him in the middle of the room, while she hurried to the closet. But even as she reached the door, she turned back and pressed on the light. Her eyes were shining. Almost breathlessly, but as softly as though it were a secret, she whispered that the war was over.

And then she was hugging and kissing him again, laughing at him because he was so puzzled, telling him, over and over again, that his father would be home now; his father had lived through it all . . . And the next thing Mark knew he was back in his room, trying to get dressed as fast as he could, but he was so excited he failed to think straight. His underwear turned inside out, and then obstinately refused to button. He couldn't find both shoes. He kept repeating to himself that he had been right, that this was a special occasion, for not only was he allowed to get up in the middle of the night, but his mother was different than she had ever been before; she was like someone at school who was playing a game. But now he couldn't find his other shoe.

Mark began to shiver. Just imagine getting up in the middle of the night! It had never happened before. He shivered again, but it was a happy shiver, for excitement was coming. Just listen to the voices from the town!

His mother kept calling him to hurry, so that, finally, he had to give up as lost his other shoe; he rushed to the front door to join his mother, with one foot still in his bedroom slipper.

They ran from the house, without shutting the door. He meant to return, but he was hurrying too fast. But almost in every house that he saw as they came nearer the town, front doors were open and blocks of light led into hallways; and everyone was hurrying. People shouted at one another; women ran up to his mother to cry how wonderful it was; she replied that it certainly was, and squeezed his hand. She was excited, too, for sometimes she started to run with him, but then stopped and held him back, and laughed.

Mark saw a man standing on the sidewalk, with his hands in the air, shouting; and another man, running up to him, grabbed his arm to shake his hand. A woman met them, and one of the men put his arms around her and lifted her into the air. He did it by pulling her against him, so that he seemed to lift her off his chest. Mark decided that he must be very strong, for he had himself once tried and was unable to lift Judith.

Now the streets ran with people. Everyone was pressing against everyone else. The bells rolled in excitement. Mark became lost in a forest of legs and hips; he held on as tightly as he could to his mother's hand, but a man and a woman, running, brushed him off the sidewalk into the gutter. As he got up, he saw the man stop and kiss the woman; then they ran on again. The woman screamed and waved her hand. Then somebody else bumped into Mark, and he fell down again.

His mother was beside him then, helping him get back on the sidewalk. An automobile came down the street, with people hanging on it and waving; the driver kept blowing the horn. A man, running toward the car, bumped into Mark and his mother, and stopped to say he was sorry.

His mother had said when they left the house that he would always remember this night, and he believed that he would, all right, for he had never seen anything like it. The town was not at all the same. There were no street lights, and the sky was more pink than blue; the people were acting as he had never known grown-ups to act before. He decided they were crazy, and he kept saying Crazy, Crazy, over and over again.

Some older fellows from the school ran by, whooping. One of them had his nightgown on under his overalls. Mark could see that, and he was shocked, for that was actually indecent, an older fellow running around in a nightgown! He ran past Mark, without looking to one side or the other, just forward, as though he had somewhere to go, and was stricken to get there.

"Why do you look so solemn?" Mark heard his mother saying. But he shook his head; he felt uneasy.

They came to the steepest part of the hill, and again he was knocked down. A man, carrying an American flag, bumped into him. "Are you all right?" the man yelled, and ran on, without waiting for Mark to reply. His mother brushed off his clothes and with her handkerchief wiped his neck. He feared for a moment that she would notice that he was on the street, in public, wearing a bedroom slipper.

Someone had a cowbell and was ringing it and shouting, and all the people seemed to be gathering at one place, as if it were the place to be, below the main street, near the railroad depot. Men were crowded around the telegraph office there. One man was standing in the yellow light of the doorway, reading from a piece of paper and saying something, again and again, about Armistice, Armistice; and each time he said it, everybody cheered.

Mark intended to ask his mother what Armistice meant, but there was too much shouting; besides, it seemed to him that she gave her son little attention. Once she even let go of his hand; that was when a woman ran up and threw her arms around her. He did not know who the woman was, either; but before he could find out, there were many people, some he knew and some he did not, crowding around his mother and laughing. He watched them, evenly, and decided that he hated them; he hated every one of them. He would walk away, and then she would be sorry.

Before he actually started, though, he saw some men running toward the railway yard, carrying armfuls of dead wood. They were running so hard and making so much noise that he abruptly decided he would stay by his mother. Then he heard crashes in the darkness, and tugged at his mother's hand until he could see what was happening. Over by the bank, near the old church, the men were ripping away a fence. Two pigeons, escaping, flew into the air, but one went the wrong way, in the dark, and struck the church door, and in terror kept striking against it until a man grabbed the pigeon.

His mother said there was going to be a bonfire, and this was the best yet. Mark felt happier. They were going to have a bonfire right there in the street!

People were shouting that the boys got the Kaiser, and the crowd laughed, for a man moved into the light carrying a scarecrow on a stick. "Here he is, boys!" the man shouted, and everyone laughed again. They had the Kaiser, and now his father would be home again. The cowbell clanged in triumph; and now Mark felt a great deal better. His mother was paying attention to him. She was trying to lift him up so that he could see the fire, but he was too heavy. All he could see was the reflection of the fire that lit up people's faces in orange flashes, and then left them dark again. But in a moment he could feel the heat; there was a crackling noise, a great cheer, and sparks fled toward the sky.

Until Mark and his mother left the street, to stand on a small hill, away from the crowd, they did not know that Mr. Anderson was in trouble. They could see him vividly by the light of the fire, down in the crowd, arguing with another man. The man held a pigeon in his hand, but the pigeon was beating its wings and struggling so hard that the man's arm was jerked one way and another, in a shower of feathers. The man was trying to hold the pigeon aloft, while he shouted, "The dove of peace! Hey, folks! The dove of peace!" People were laughing.

But Mr. Anderson grabbed the man by the arm, and in the struggle, as they both stumbled into the crowd, the pigeon escaped and flew fast and wild, away from the fire and into the dark.

The crowd moved forward, shouting. The man was swinging his fists at Mr. Anderson, but some-one grabbed him. Mark stared, fascinated. He had never known until then that grown-ups had fights, and now his old friend Mr. Anderson was having a fight. His mother was tugging at his hand, but he begged to stay; and before she dragged him away, he saw the janitor of the school climb up on the wood pile by the fire, where he stood waving his hands for quiet. Mark could not hear what he said, but he kept pointing at Mr. Anderson as he spoke. The crowd shoved backward and forward, and his mother and he were hemmed in by people behind them.

Mark could tell that Mr. Anderson was trying to get away and that some men kept dragging him back to the fire. Mr. Anderson's hat fell off and he groped along the ground for it; someone picked it up and pulled it down over his head. Then everyone laughed, because the men had boosted him to the top of the wood pile, alongside the janitor, who was still talking. Mr. Anderson stood up straight and brushed off his clothes; then he turned away from the janitor and started to climb down. But they threw him back again; he landed on his knees, his coat up over his face. Now the crowd was suddenly quiet, and Mark heard a man in the dark shout, "The war's over, for Christ's sakes!"

There were cries of alarm, and then the janitor shouted, "All right, but if he can deny it, let him!" Mr. Anderson must have said something, for Mark heard the janitor call him a God-damned pro-German liar. "That's all I got to say," he said, "that's all I got to say."

And then Mr. Anderson got to his feet, and stood facing the crowd. It was so quiet that Mark could hear his own heart beating like a drum within him. His mother was trying to drag him away. The flames crackled and hissed.

Then something happened that he could not understand. The crowd was very quiet, daylight was coming, and Mr. Anderson still stood there, as though over all a moment was suspended. If he spoke, Mark did not hear him. All he saw, looking back, was Mr. Anderson standing there for a long time, trying to speak. And when the moment was over, his head bowed, so that Mark could see only his hat and beard above the crowd. Everyone seemed to be laughing.

And when Mark turned to his mother in bewilderment, he saw that her eyes were filled with tears.

A strange week passed, one in which everyone talked of Armistice night and of Mr. Anderson. Poor man, they said. And yet it was a week of much happiness, for there were many visitors and ice-cream parties. Mark scarcely knew his mother, she seemed to have such a good time. She danced with him and warned him that he had better be an extra good boy, for his father was coming home. "Of course," she said, "of course, he will bring you a present!"

At first his mother had been fearful of the crowd's effect upon Mark, for she forgot that he had no understanding of that kind of pain. The feeling in him that she believed horror, was really his complete confusion, for he had never seen a man crying before. If he had any terror at all, it was when he thought he might meet Mr. Anderson, for now he would not know how to act in his presence. Something had happened to Mr. Anderson that he could not understand; and he must, therefore, avoid him.

Eighteenth Chapter

Now CHRISTMAS was very near. His mother had made certain errands and there were drawers that he could not touch. The writing table had bright cards and tinsel in a splash of color, and in the basement a fir tree waited impatiently.

There had been tears one evening when his mother learned that his father could not return by Christmas, but a package had already been sent to France, and there would be one in return anyday now. But one small trouble remained for Mark. School would begin just before Christmas, and continue right up to that day. That was because of the long suspension in the term during the influenza plague. Still, Mark did not mind as much as he pretended to; it would be good to return to school next Monday, even though Christmas followed directly after.

Indeed, it had now become exciting to go almost anywhere, and particularly to the store. Not only the sights, but the sounds and the smells, too, made it so. New packages of figs and dates, in bright red and green wrappers, were on the counters and shelves. The coffee grinder would be going, and the grocer would be slicing citron; and nuts and apples lay in great sacks in the corners. There was the bright ring of the cash drawer, and the stiff, dry smell of new overalls.

And of course upstairs in that store there were tables of toys; one table alone of cowboy suits and cap pistols, and another with soldier suits and of machine guns that fired wooden bullets, a dozen bullets to a belt. There were new boots for boys just his size, and raincoats with oilskin helmets the shape of firemen's hats, alongside of baseball suits with heavy red sweaters. Mechanical sets with real screwdrivers and metal braces were everywhere, in a wonderful confusion of bolts and screws and designs for bridges. But best of all was a brown truck-line machine, a miniature army tank on real rubber wheels. The tank was almost the size of a crackerbox, and it was so wonderful to behold that it would be the best present of all.

Even in town the weather was wintry. There was no snow, but frost had come in all its stealth to freeze the ground hard. In the night, when the imperious wind came down from the mountains, Mark could hear the pine trees crack and bend; in their indignation, they dropped pine cones on the roof of his house and made him glad he was in bed.

These days it was good to be in the house even in the daytime, for there everything dozed in the heat of the furnace. Outside the cold air made you feel like running, but you were always glad to get back in the house again.

While school was still suspended and the weather was too cold for playing outside, he and his mother often visited together in the afternoons; he was the guest who came from upstairs to see her. They had been playing games ever since the war ended. She said she never imagined, really, that anything would have happened to his father; but it was good now to know that nothing had.

They were in the dining room one afternoon fixing a package for a person his mother called Aunt Carol. He had tried, but he was unable to recall her. His mother brought him the photograph album to show him her picture, and they spent most of the afternoon looking at it. "This is your Uncle Bob and here is his wife Carol." She held the album up to the window so that he could see it easier. The book was filled with people whom he did not know. "This is Doctor Will. See, he's with your cousin. She was a baby then—and here are the three of them together, Maude, and Doctor Will, and your cousin." Mark looked at them curiously; they were his relatives, strange, stiff-looking people, all faded and brown, with dim houses and hills in the distance.

He turned the page and came upon a picture of narrow, dark houses, tall but close together, in a street rather narrow. "What's that?" he asked. "Oh, that's where your father lived before he came here. That's the East. I was there, but I was almost too young to remember it." Mark had never seen such a place, houses so close together and so much alike. He imagined the East surely must be a strange place. It was not really the East, like China, for it was in America and it was a nearer kind of East.

On the next page was a picture of his father and mother, but they looked so different he disliked the picture. His father had his hair combed funny; he was holding his hat in his hand and his other arm was around Mark's mother. In a second photograph they stood before a baby carriage. "And in that," his mother said, raising her voice, "is a young person you ought to know . . . That was taken when we went to the ocean, but I guess you don't remember that, do you?"

She showed him still another picture of himself as a baby, but he did not recognize himself at all. He looked like any other baby.

"Here you are again—at thirteen months," she said, "and here's you at two years," but he was not a bit interested until he came to a photograph that had not yet been glued to the page. He caught his breath, for here he was in a soldier suit, in Richard's helmet! Mark glowed in self-admiration; he was sure he looked just like a soldier.

His mother then turned to the front of the book and showed him some pictures taken of her when she was a child. Mark saw a thin little girl, straight and long-legged, with a ribbon in her hair. This girl was scarcely his mother. Except for her dress and the way her hair was fixed, she might have been Judith, or someone at school. "Are you sure it's you?" he said.

But his mother turned some more pages, and then he saw some pictures that looked like her. Her hair was gathered around her head so that short curls fell over her forehead. Her wide-apart eyes stared resolutely into the camera, but the expression on her face was startled, as if the photographer had tricked her, but in doing so had caught her beauty. "That was just before I was married," his mother told him.

And on the next page she was wearing the same dress, but a man was with her. He was Mr. Blake, but he seemed thinner and taller, and his lips were pressed together. "I dared him to smile," Mark heard his mother saying. In the picture her own face was almost turned completely away from the camera. In the background was a tree, and behind it, a lawn. The lawn was deep and the tree so thick with foliage that Mark thought the picture must have been taken somewhere away from Colburn, in the East or at the ocean, for outside his window now the trees were bare and the grass was gone, and it was so cold outside there was a mist upon the windows.

"But that was taken in the summertime," his mother said. "It's at the old Blake place. There's the arbor in the back. I used to trim it when I lived with the Blakes."

Now out of the dark of his memory, Mark suddenly recalled a conversation he had long ago in Richard's kitchen. "Mother," he said, in surprise, turning to her, "did you ever step out with Mr. Blake?"

"What!" she said.

Slightly alarmed by her tone, he repeated the question very slowly. "Did you?" he urged her.

She looked at him for a moment, and then he saw she was laughing at him. "Did you?" he asked, again.

"Where in the world did you ever get that idea?" she said.

Mark only partly remembered. "That's what they said," he told her. He was defensive; when she laughed at him, he felt uneasy. "Olaf said so. That's what Olaf said."

His mother wanted to know what Olaf said. "You mean Christina's son?" she asked.

"In Richard's kitchen," Mark told her, trying to remember that far back, "when we were in Richard's kitchen, Olaf came in and he said that's what—that you used to step out with Mr. Blake, and what that meant was that you were going to marry him, Mr. Blake I mean, but then he would have been my father." Mark finished in a rush of words, trying to stop his mother from laughing at him.

"Olaf's crazy, I guess," he added.

"Well," she said, straightening up in her chair, "the young man certainly doesn't know what he's talking about, and neither do you . . . I wish you would quit using that horrid expression—'step-out,' I mean."

Mark repeated, stubbornly, that it was what Olaf had said.

"I hope," he heard his mother saying, "that you weren't as frank as this with James Blake. You didn't say anything about this to him, did you?"

Mark replied that he had not. "And don't," she said.

Then his mother said, "I guess what Olaf meant was that I used to live with the Blakes when I was a girl, and that we were raised together." Mark nodded. "Well," she said, "as I told you, we were raised together, or at least part of the time when my father had to travel all over the West for the railroad companies. Between trips he stayed with us." She opened the album. "See, here's his picture. Isn't he the pleasantest man you ever saw?"

Mark saw a familiar face, a person he knew. He saw a round little man, in a great dark coat and a high collar; he was fingering his watch-chain and smiling into the camera. Mark knew him, but he likewise knew that his grandfather was dead. That was all he knew about him.

He heard his mother say, "Oh, Mark, I loved him. I counted the days between his trips. He was nearer to me than most fathers, I suppose, because

I can scarcely remember my mother. But he was wonderful, Mark."

Mark felt sad, but his mother squeezed his arm, and turned the pages to show him some more pictures.

"Did you go to school when you lived there?" Mark asked.

"In the Blake house, you mean? I lived there until I married your father. We lived in the city, at first, until this house was built and your father could practice. Then we came back here, and you were born."

"Was I?" he said, eagerly.

"Yes," she replied. "Fancy that!"

Mark was happy to think about it.

"Mr. Anderson and his wife were the first people to live up here," she told him, "and we came second. Then when poor old Uncle Blake passed away, James Blake and his wife came up here."

"With Judith," Mark was going to shout, but just in time he remembered. He walked over to his mother's side. "Show me my picture in the soldier's suit again," he said.

They were looking at the album and laughing when they were interrupted by a sound at the front door; someone was using the knocker, instead of the bell. The knocker was there just for decoration. The knocker sounded again. His mother looked at Mark and lifted her eyebrows. He watched her take off her apron and run to the door.

"Oh, Mr. Anderson," he heard her say. "Come in, we were just speaking of you." Mark jumped up, ready to run to his friend, but then he felt frightened. He would not know how to act in front of him. Besides, Mr. Anderson had not come to his house for a long time.

Mark heard his mother calling him from the hallway, and he walked into the parlor very slowly. Mr. Anderson was carrying a package, a rather large package, almost the size of a wooden crackerbox. And Mr. Anderson looked different. Mark did not know exactly why; he just looked different. His beard was brushed back and his hair was neatly combed, and he was wearing a dark blue suit that made him look uncomfortable. He heard his mother ask Mr. Anderson to bring his things into the hall, and then Mark saw that Mr. Anderson had left his overcoat and a straw suitcase out on the porch.

Mr. Anderson cleared his throat and coughed. "I just have a minute, Mrs. Douglas. Just a minute." He paused, and then said in regular phrases, "I just dropped in with this package for I am leaving on the afternoon train. I just wanted to drop in to say goodbye to you and Mark and to thank you for all the good things you and your husband have done for me, because I am leaving this afternoon for Idaho."

"You are moving away?" his mother asked.

"Oh yes," he replied, "I have given up the farm." Mark stared at him, until Mr. Anderson looked at him and smiled.

"I am sorry to hear that," his mother said. "I know that Mark will miss you a great deal."

Mr. Anderson was still looking at him. "Mark and me have been good friends," he said, and winked at him. And after a pause, he added, "I have a sister in Idaho. I will be glad to see her."

"In Idaho," Mark heard his mother repeating. "Mrs. Perkins comes from Idaho, you know. I hear it's very nice."

Mr. Anderson nodded. Idaho was the end of the world. "Well, Mark," he said, after a pause, "you're getting to be a big boy."

"Almost as big as a fifth grader!" Mark turned to his mother for confirmation, but Mr. Anderson gave it to him first. "You are that, Mark," he said.

He was still holding the package. He glanced from Mark to his mother, and then took out his watch. "Excuse me," he said, "I've just got a minute." He put the package on a chair. "If you don't mind," he said, "this is for Mark."

And as soon as he said that, Mark forgot his uneasiness. He ran to the package and shouted, "It's an army tank!" He wanted to see the tank right away.

But his mother said that he should not open it until Christmas. "Perhaps," she said, "Mr. Anderson wants you to put it away until then."

"No, mam," Mr. Anderson replied, "it's not a Christmas present. It's just something I'd like the boy to have. It isn't much, and it isn't new, and I guess it won't be much for him now, but when he gets older he can use it for his studying." He paused, and looked from one to the other. "It's a dictionary," he said.

Mark did not know what he meant. Mr. Anderson said, "It won't be much use for him now, I guess."

"How fine!" Mark's mother said.

"He can open it now," Mr. Anderson reassured her. "I just used the box to carry it over. He can open it now, if he wants to."

Mark tried to open the package, but his mother had to help him with it. She seemed to think it was a fine present. "Isn't that fine?" she kept saying. "The large, complete one, too!"

Mark thanked Mr. Anderson for it. Then he lifted the cover of the book to sneak a look at the inside, but it was just a lot of small printing. But Mark knew by now that he must pretend he liked it. He thanked Mr. Anderson again, and then tried to lift the book. But it was almost too heavy; his mother helped him carry it to the table.

"This is so thoughtful of you," his mother kept saying. "It's a gift he'll always appreciate." Mr. Anderson was moving toward the door, moving his hat in his hands.

"Come say good-bye to Mr. Anderson," his mother said to Mark. He shook hands with him, but Mr. Anderson's hand was so large his own almost felt lost in it. It was hardly like a hand at all; it was rough and hard.

Then his mother had shaken hands with Mr. Anderson. "You will write us?" she said.

"I will remember you," Mr. Anderson said, evenly. And the last sight Mark had of him was when he picked up his suitcase and walked away.

Back in the house, his mother leaned with her back against the closed door for a moment and looked at Mark across the room. He saw her look into the mirror and with both hands brush her hair back from the sides of her head. Then she walked over to the table and looked at the dictionary, and he followed her. On the first page there was some writing in ink, and she read it to him.

"To Mark," she said, "from his good friend— Carl Anderson."

Carl Anderson. Mark looked at the signature. It seemed strange that he was Carl Anderson instead of Mr. Anderson. The page was brown around the edges. He turned another page and looked at the pictures of some flags.

His mother took the book from him and carried it over to the sofa. He came over by her. "Will you read me what he said again?" he asked her, for it was not written very clearly.

Mark opened the book near the front, and found another page with a lot of writing on it. "What does this say?" he asked, but she was already reading it.

"Luise Elsa Anderson, née Boehn," she said, "married June Seventh, Eighteen-hundred and Eighty-seven, in Springfield, Illinois."

In another ink, but as faded, was the entry:

"Carl Boehn Anderson, born at five A.M. February Second, Eighteen-hundred and Eighty-nine; died February Fifth of that year."

And below it, the final entry:

"Luise Elsa Anderson (born in Frankfort, Germany, April Twenty-first, Eighteen-hundred and Sixty-seven), died January Fourth, Nineteen-hundred and Twelve. A faithful wife and friend for twenty-five years."

His mother closed the book, and put her arms around him. "Religious people use the Bible," she said. She pulled him very close to her, until he couldn't see her face. "He gave it to you, Mark— to the youngest person he knew." Her arms tightened around him. "Oh, Mark!" she said.

"What's the matter, Mother?" he asked.

"Nothing," she told him, "nothing." And there was really nothing the matter. She was only crying a little.

Later that evening Mark asked his mother if Mr. Anderson would ever come back. "Not even for Christmas!" he exclaimed, for he thought that was too bad. He asked her what would happen to Mr. Anderson's farm, but she said he had given it back to the bank. But she smiled at him when he wondered if the bank would take it away, too.

For it seemed to Mark that everything was ending at once, and now people were gone or going away.

They said the war was over, and so was the influenza. He wondered what would happen to him, but then in delight he remembered that Christmas was coming. And he would go back to school.

Nineteenth Chapter

THIS IS the end of the story, then, and yet in a way it is the beginning. Looking back on the boy from the height of time, the man he became saw him returning in December to the cycle he had begun one morning in September.

In the boy's life more than a month had passed since the end of the war. There was the promise that his father would be home in the first month of the New Year. And now that the influenza had come and gone in its inexplicable course, there had been many days of sunshine, so that the robes of grief were seen less often in the streets. Even school was to begin. The newspaper had said so; there were new books and pencils, and even the desks had been revarnished. Christmas itself was so near that he could touch it, and one day now led straightly to another. If there had been a dislocation in time, the world once more in its wonderful fashion was turning around and around, the same as ever.

Once again the day was Monday, and in the early hours of morning the town patiently awaited the great event. Even the earth was swept clean, for during the night invisible forces had been at work cleaning the countryside, thoughtfully keeping in mind that at daylight their job must be done, the earth ready for the children's commotion. The old leaves of autumn, once crimson, were tucked into the obscure corners; the trees were left washed and bare in the early light, and the glare was gone from the blue winter's sky, so that it hung overhead like an upturned saucer, as mottled and opaque as porcelain thoroughly scrubbed.

In time the kitchens had fires, pans rattled on the stoves, and the morning breezes began to smell of toast. A long sleep, and now the hour had come. Doors slammed, and in their escape from their houses the children shouted, running from their yards and calling to friends in joy and a kind of derision. The stores had opened and automobiles slipped by along the road. Up on the hill, near Mark's house, the wooden wheels of the farm wagons creaked over the hard ground, indicating the sort of commerce that had begun.

Mark felt very good again, on his way to school. Swaddled in clothing, but cold with excitement, he kicked at the curb to warm his toes and to show that he was happy. He was walking up the long hill, in a triumphant march over its fine cement sidewalk. He would have an exciting day; he would have a new teacher, someone he had never seen before. He would see Mr. Blake, and Mr. Blake would be glad to see him.

His mother had warned him that not all the pupils he had known would be present, but even while she was speaking he was not as sad as he could be, for he thought there might be some new ones. And if there were, he would extend them his pity, for they would know far less than he did. He was able to read and write, in a certain fashion. Even the signs in the streets spoke words to him. TEN MILES PER HOUR—STOP—SLOW UP, CURVE; he knew all that. And just this morning his mother had given him a pair of gloves, for he had become too old for mittens. Soon he would be in the second grade, when life kept its promise.

Oh, this was a wonderful day! In school he would beam and smile, and learn all his lessons, and in no time at all he would have the Gold Star. He would be good friends with Richard, and never again would he fight anyone who was his friend. That was the way to do; that was the way to be like other people . . . Walking along, thinking in this manner, Mark paused now and then to nod to an imaginary fellow, to whom he was explaining these difficult matters. He gestured with his hands, so that his friend could see his fine red gloves.

Older now, Mark was no longer interested in the oak tree or its acorns. He was so busy that he passed the tree by. Not only that, but when he came to the meadow he ignored the geese. He knew they were there, but they were not now as they once had been. Indeed, when Mark saw them he scarcely hurried at all.

The heavy clouds of winter were filling the sky, but they were not important enough, either, to call his attention. Muffled in his thoughts, he walked along without seeing the earth or the sky. He remembered Judith, and that she had once been afraid of the geese, and he was sorry now that Judith was not with him. He would have helped her past them.

Before Mark knew he had gone so far, he came to the long white line of picket fences, shining with the morning dew. They were his old friends, and he let his finger touch each one as he walked along, without thinking of what he was doing. Yet even a passing touch gave him reassurance. But the damp came through, awakening him from his vagary. His fine gloves were stained, and that made him very angry. He stopped and stared at the fence, letting his head lower slowly until he was in a fighting position. Then he stepped forward and gave the fence a kick, and thus got his revenge. He was still angry, though, for how could he be a good boy when even the fences were in league with the wet, when even the dew tried to get him into trouble?

Mark kicked the fence another time. "That for you," he said, "that and that for you." One for the fence and one for the wet.

But even while he spoke, the sky had become

much darker. A wind crept over the hill and caught him when he was not looking. Then the rain began to fall, lightly at first, as though in a gentle rebuke; but Mark said nothing. Then it came harder and harder, until it beat about him, tearing at his clothes and hissing in his ears. The thunder itself spoke once. Mark was already hurrying as fast as he could; his lips were pressed together, yet once he said out loud what was in his mind that moment. "I didn't mean to do it! I didn't mean to do it!" But to whom he was speaking, he did not know. Now the rain was getting even.

Memory brings the scene. The boy fled from the storm as he did that first day in September, as if the wind and the rain held between them a time in his life, and he could sprint from one horizon to the other. That time was almost complete in itself, as deep and clear as it was deceptive, but even then his memory had been forever wedded to water, for the man he became remembered the day but forgot an enormous night. He had imagined that his childhood was the safest place, and that in it there was nothing worse to run from than the rain.

The boy at the time knew better. As soon as the first drops struck him, he ran toward school and shelter; out of his childhood, running as fast as he was able.

CPSIA information can be obtained
at www.ICGtesting.com
Printed in the USA
LVOW02s0424281215

468054LV00012B/220/P